STRIKING REVIEWS FOR CHRIS OFFUTT AND
The Same River Twice

"In this memoir of the decade . . . Chris Offutt picks up where Daniel Boone left off, thumbing his way out of Appalachia in search of new frontiers." —*The New Yorker*

"[Chris Offutt] is a potent new American writer with a beautiful voice." —Kim McLaurin, *The Houston Post Book World*

"Somewhere on the road . . . Mr. Offutt learned to tell stories, which [he] does exquisitely . . . rich and fantastic and desperately honest." —Sue Halpern, *The New York Times Book Review*

"[Offutt's] journey is a classic. . . . In a world that is sometimes dangerous, usually depressing and perpetually grimy—also a world darkly humorous—one remembers his story as one of restoration and reconciliation, redemption and rebirth." —Brad Knickerbocker, *The Christian Science Monitor*

"His memoir marks the debut of a wonderful new talent. . . . Offutt has the sharpest eye and most potent style of the several talented writers to recently come out of coal country." —D. T. Max, *New York Newsday*

"Memorable . . . [Offutt's] tale should be looked at as the tale of a generation that came of age in the late '70s." —Tim McLaurin, *The Washington Post*

"Offutt the diarist has no models. *The Same River Twice* is a wild original . . . [displaying] the nihilistic passivity of a graduate student with the physical robustness of a convict." —*St. Petersburg Times*

"There sometimes creeps into the tone of memoirs a voice too sincere, too literal in intention, to capture the narrative freedom that fiction allows. But Chris Offutt finds an angle of entry that loosens things up . . . [and] achieves an amazing closure." —Vince Passaro, *Mirabella*

PENGUIN BOOKS

THE SAME RIVER TWICE

Chris Offutt was born in 1958 and grew up in the Appalachian region of eastern Kentucky. His stories have appeared in *Esquire* and other literary magazines, and his work has received an NEA grant and a James Michener grant. He is the author of the story collection *Kentucky Straight*. He lives with his wife and two sons.

The
Same
River
Twice

A Memoir

CHRIS OFFUTT

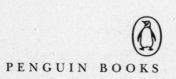

PENGUIN BOOKS

PENGUIN BOOKS
Published by the Penguin Group
Penguin Books USA Inc., 375 Hudson Street,
New York, New York 10014, U.S.A.
Penguin Books Ltd, 27 Wrights Lane, London W8 5TZ, England
Penguin Books Australia Ltd, Ringwood, Victoria, Australia
Penguin Books Canada Ltd, 10 Alcorn Avenue,
Toronto, Ontario, Canada M4V 3B2
Penguin Books (N.Z.) Ltd, 182–190 Wairau Road,
Auckland 10, New Zealand

Penguin Books Ltd, Registered Offices:
Harmondsworth, Middlesex, England

First published in the United States of America by
Simon & Schuster, Inc., 1993
Published in Penguin Books 1994

10 9 8 7 6 5 4 3 2 1

The lines from "The Town We Know and Leave Behind, The Rivers We
Carry With Us" are reprinted from *White Center: Poems* by Richard Hugo,
by permission of W. W. Norton & Company, Inc. Copyright © 1980
by Richard Hugo.

THE LIBRARY OF CONGRESS HAS CATALOGUED THE HARDCOVER AS FOLLOWS:
Offutt, Chris.
The same river twice: a memoir/Chris Offutt.
p.   cm.
ISBN 0-671-78734-9 (hc.)
ISBN 0 14 02.3253 2 (pbk.)
1. Offutt, Chris.   2. United States—Biography.   I. Title.
CT275.035A3 1993
973—dc20 [B]

Printed in the United States of America
Set in Baskerville
Designed by Songhee Kim

For

Rita, Sam and James

I forget the names of towns without rivers.
A town needs a river to forgive the town.
Whatever river, whatever town—
It is much the same.
The cruel things I did, I took to the river.
I begged the current: make me better.

—*Richard Hugo,* "THE
TOWNS WE KNOW AND LEAVE
BEHIND, THE RIVERS WE CARRY
WITH US"

Prologue

The midwestern land has a softly undulating quality, like concentric circles spreading from a rock tossed into a farm pond. Before the giant plowing icebergs, water covered everything here. Often I see the bottom of an ancient ocean quite clearly—the ripples left by forgotten tides, the gentle upsweeps of a reef—and I imagine that the land is still under water. I possess gills in the woods and move against the resistance, exploring an abandoned sea.

Cloud shadows are great fish moving swiftly overhead. The prairie disappears into the glare of refracted sunlight fading with the depth, and becomes the living floorboards of an ocean. Jet contrails in the sky are a ship's prow, cleaving the surface far away. Breath bubbles around my head as movement slows. Sound drifts into silence. I have slid out of my century and into an undersea past, alone with an uncaring force.

I am as alien here as in a city. I don't belong, none of us does. Thumb and cranium lucked us into our current status and we've traded curiosity for erosion. Dinosaurs evolved until their bodies were too big for their brains and they could not command their limbs. The human mind has outstripped its body—we are as ungainly as the last great lizard.

The rivers of the nation are only water now, no longer rivers in any sense, trickles mostly, filled with poison. In ten million years a stranger will explore this former sea, this former iceberg, this former prairie, and sift through our remains. Instead of spear points and mastodon bones he will find bits of plastic. I should be a rock sculptor, carving a mighty pantheon to rival the debris we left on the moon. The ashes of Alexander's library reveal the fragility of books.

M y arrival in Iowa coincided with a two-year drought that left stunted corn drooping dead in the field. Brown grass crackled underfoot. The shadeless terrain reminded me of cheap plywood warped from too much time in weather. Temperatures at night surpassed a hundred. After my years of living in cities and mountains, the prairie offered me the unique ability to see trouble coming a long way off.

Rita and I rented, a small house along the Iowa River. Due to zoning laws and the risk of flood, people owned their homes but not the land. Many of the houses were built on skids to be pulled by a bulldozer in case of eviction. Our dirt road ran parallel to the river past a wire fence thick with lopped-off catfish heads. Thirty acres of forest surrounded us. I took a long walk in the floodplain woods every day.

The locals accepted my presence; the state has long been known for tolerance. Public poker is legal at low stakes and motorcycle helmets are not required. Iowa is host to Amish and Mennonites, a large band of Maharishi folk, and the communal farms of the Amana colonies. Everyone has lived through drought, tornado, hail, blizzard, and fierce winds that scream across the prairie for hundreds of miles. There are two seasons—hot and cold. With any luck, autumn lasts a week; spring but a single afternoon.

There is no national park in Iowa, and if its state parks were stitched together, they'd occupy a space less than ten miles square. Ninety-five percent of the land is given over to agriculture, the highest of any state. Iowans wrestle, read, play miniature golf, and fly scale model aircraft—pastimes that require little ground space. Manned balloons drift every summer sky. Farmers have used the land so long that the richest soil in the nation is just old dirt, requiring a variety of chemicals that stay in the earth. Tap water cannot be trusted.

I was born and raised on a ridge in Eastern Kentucky, in the middle of the Daniel Boone National Forest. Trees grew close together, tangled with dense undergrowth. A greater variety of flora and fauna coexisted there than anywhere else in the country. I spent most of my childhood in those woods. Half of what I know, I learned there alone. At nineteen I left, vowing always to own my time. What began as an adherence to freedom became an inability to hold a job.

Five years ago, the night the Red Sox won the pennant, I'd asked Rita to marry me. We were drinking in a crowded Boston bar. She refused, and I was grateful, needing time to examine my shocking and spontaneous request. The second time was on a weekend trip to a cabin in upstate New York. We visited a lake where her family had vacationed when she was a girl. Surrounded by the roar of a waterfall, I asked her again, and she said no. This bothered me since I'd thought about it and I was sober.

"No, you're not," she said. "You're drunk on nature."

Being refused twice led me to a careful strategy, guaranteed to catch her when she was weak. On the morning of her birthday, I hurried to the bathroom ahead of her. A few minutes later she stumbled into my trap. We were both nude. I eased my knees to the cold tile. "Happy birthday," I said. "Will you marry me?" Bleary-eyed and half asleep, she said yes, and stepped past me to the toilet.

We were wed in Manhattan, Rita's hometown, at the Municipal Building on Chambers Street. The facility was undergoing renovation and the actual chapel was closed. We used an auxiliary room that contained a scaffolding, tools, and a dropcloth. Ahead of us in line was an Asian couple; just behind us, a Hispanic couple. We all served as one another's witnesses, though none of us spoke a common tongue. Our ceremony lasted two minutes, long enough for the justice of the peace to drop one of the mismatched rings I'd bought in a Hell's Kitchen pawnshop. His clumsiness was understandable since I'd sprinkled a handful of soil on the floor. It was from my family home and I wanted to stand on it for the ceremony.

We moved to Kentucky shortly thereafter, and to Iowa a year later. The subject of children became a frequent though vague topic between us. Rita worked as a psychologist, providing care for the homeless and mentally ill. I was trying to be a writer—with her financial support. This meant abandoning twelve years of diligent journal entries for what I considered "real writing." A child struck me as the one ingredient that would ruin my hopes, forcing me into full-time employment. I told her this was the wrong time. She pointed out that there was no right time.

"Besides," she said, "I'm thirty-four."

I'd always wanted kids, but figured it wouldn't be fair to them since I could barely support myself. On the other hand, I was thirty-three years old, the age when Jesus died, when Alexander had conquered the known world. My youth was behind me, not misspent exactly, but squandered to a certain extent. While the rest of my generation had been lodging themselves into careers, I'd pretty much run amok.

Rita was smart enough not to push the idea of a child. It was always there, though, shimmering between us, sometimes off to the side, intangible but strong. I'd catch her looking at a woman pushing a baby carriage, and feel a vague guilt, as if I were denying her. I studied fathers in town with their kids, trying to imagine myself in their position. The men seemed out of sorts, like tourists in a strange port, self-conscious of their foreign clothes. Invariably there passed between father and child a private moment that filled me with awe.

I told a few fathers that my wife wanted a baby and I was edgy. Their responses were always the same—"A lot of work, but worth it," and, "Nothing is ever the same again." I nodded without comprehension. They could have been talking about the construction of a hydroelectric dam that would give unknown power to a small community. All I could see was what I'd lose.

I began gauging Rita as a potential mother, seeking flaws, some hidden impediment that would give rise to psychopathic progeny. Unfortunately, she passed muster. Her chief drawback was considering me fit material for paternity, a flattering fault. She loved me and wanted a family. I'm not afraid of much, and it bothered me that I was scared of something as basic as having a child. The subject remained with us, floating like an ovum waiting for a sperm.

In autumn, a terrible awareness crept through my mind, moving with the certitude of a saboteur. There was a limit to Rita's childbearing years. If I genuinely loved her, I'd have to leave her. Worse, I had to leave her soon. She needed enough time to find a man who wanted a family. Considering it from this angle was like weighing options on a scale—a life alone without her, or a life with Rita and a child. The decision was remarkably simple. I went to town and got drunk.

The next day was smudged by a vicious hangover, a haze that stood between the world and me. When Rita came home from work, I asked her to join me at the kitchen table, where I'd placed her diaphragm, tube of jelly, and my emergency condoms. One by one, I dropped everything in the garbage. Rita's eyes were damp. She was smiling. There began my true education, after years of practice, in the ways of flesh. Sex with the goal of conception finally meant making love. The chief difficulty lay in shedding my adolescent fear of knocking her up.

After a winter of delirious sex with no fecundity, we were nervous that something was wrong. In early spring I began watching nature for clues. When ducks mated along the river, three males went after one female and they very nearly drowned her. She was left dazed in the shallows. The males flew casually away, their wings dimpling the surface of the water on each downstroke. I preferred the constancy of the great blue herons, bonding in pairs and returning yearly to the same nest.

Each month, Rita anxiously waited for her period, then cried when it came. She called the doctor, who told us to keep working, that during the peak of ovulation, fertilization fails three times out of four. A woman releases fewer than four hundred eggs in her lifetime. The average man makes a thousand sperm per second. Three or four good ejaculations was enough to populate the entire world, but I couldn't get my own wife pregnant.

To allay concerns for my manhood, I read several books on conception. An illustration of fallopian tubes looked like the horned skull of a steer hanging from a neighbor's barn. Ovulation was described as "an intra-abdominal event." Ejaculation speeds reached two hundred inches per second, with sperm receiving a glucose bath by the female body for extra energy. The sperm spat enzymes to break down the wall of the nearest egg adrift from the ovary. When one finally drilled through the egg's outer shell, a trapdoor slammed shut behind it. I visualized everything happening on a large scale with accompanying sound effects and cheering, as in the Olympics.

Another guide, less technical, informed me that male orgasm fired an armada of three hundred million soldiers upriver to invade the cervix. Only one percent made it past the yoni's fierce beach. Half of these were captured and held in the zona pellucida. Prisoners had eight hours to fertilize or starve to death. The egg carried food to sustain itself, but the sperm traveled light for greater speed.

I spent an entire weekend staring silently at the river, worried that my army was composed of lazy draftees. Years of drug abuse had so confused my sperm that they couldn't swim a straight line. Rita suggested I consult our doctor, who assured me that I manufactured fresh goods every ninety days. "Think of it as a mom-and-pop store," she said. "Low overhead with a quick turnover."

She gave Rita a thermometer and a chart to monitor her ovulation. I began to wear boxer shorts. I'd read that the men of primitive cultures dipped their testicles in boiling water as a means of birth control; it seemed possible that the inverse might hold true. I filled a coffee cup with ice water and stared at it a full hour, never quite summoning the courage for immersion.

My next trip to the library yielded a pop-up book about conception. A gigantic lingam sprang from the pages, followed by a yoni the size of an animal den. The centerfold offered a huge multilevel egg. The sperm were tiny by comparison, except for one monster that dived into a slot when you opened and closed the book. The text said it was sinking its payload.

I am not by nature a squeamish man, but that pop-up book made me feel like a person who'd looked on the face of God—bewildered, regretful, possessor of forbidden knowledge. I took a long walk in the floodplain woods. A turtle rooted along a sandy bend in the river, hunting a spot to lay her eggs. I was envious until I realized we were both in the same fix—animal sex is only a billion and a half years old. I went home and threw the graph and thermometer in the trash. Turtles don't need maps. They're just slow.

On the first warm night of April, Rita and I drove to town and scaled the chain-link fence that enclosed the public swimming pool. I lurked in the shallows and watched for the law while Rita performed a flip off the high board. Her underwear flashed white against the black sky, a lovely sight, as if Virgo had become a mobile constellation, descending to earth with a graceful splash. We left the pool for a clump of shadowed oaks in the park. The sweet grass adhered to our limbs. I felt like Zeus field-testing his swan suit before the seduction of Leda. Gamete met zygote. DNA merged into the corkscrew that resembled the Milky Way's spiral, Hermes' Staff, the swift helix of infant birth.

Two weeks later Rita called from the doctor's office. She spoke fast, her voice husky with tears and glory. The test was positive. I went outside and lay down beside the river. Blue dragonflies were mating so hard they rattled dry weeds. The land seemed to recede beneath me, leaving me prone in the air, as if residing between sky and earth. The clouds moved like surf. I was stationary while all existence was on the glide.

I never thought I'd be married, let alone mutate into a father. Such normal events had never seemed to have a place in my life. To mark the occasion, I bought an aluminum skiff with a six-horse-power engine, and dubbed it Lily, Rita's middle name. I moored it in the river twenty yards from the house and felt a little better prepared for fatherhood.

Throughout April, the river rose and fell, so controlled by a dam that it was barely a river except to the fox that stalked its bank. When the sound of a dying duck crossed the water at night, I thought of that old tree falling when no one's there, and understood that regardless of listeners, the fox would kill a duck. In the same way, I realized that the baby really would be born.

We began seeing other pregnant women in town. Like locusts, they were emerging in warm weather. Rita felt the kinship of sisterhood, while I enjoyed a strange pride, as if responsible for all pregnancy. It was a potent sensation that lasted until the first of our monthly appointments with the doctor. I wanted desperately to be involved, but felt superfluous, a specialist who'd done his duty. There was so much focus on Rita that I became envious. Toward the end of each appointment, I'd invent some imaginary ailment to ask the doctor about. She always rolled her eyes, winked at Rita, and pronounced me fine.

Rita's appetite for food increased, and I responded by drinking for two. After she went to bed, I drove to a bar and shot pool with the same fervor I had in Kentucky, staking my identity on each game. Younger women grouped around Rita like acolytes hoping for insight. They were flirtatious with me, as if impending fatherhood made me safe, no longer a sexual threat. There were twenty-four thousand genes inside Rita's womb, forming a kid that was half me, a quarter my parents and so on. Going back a mere thirty-two generations gives each person over four billion ancestors, more people than currently dwelt on earth. The responsibility to procreate was over. All I had to do was guide it through the next eighteen years, the task of life.

One night a waning gibbous moon drowned the river with light. A barred owl yelled for company and I stepped into the yard to mimic its eight high-pitched cries that ended in a gurgle. The owl hollered back, closer. We repeated ourselves twice more, until the owl recognized my foreign accent and cast a disdainful silence through the darkness. In the morning, I told Rita of my worry that our child would treat me in the same manner. She patted the bulge in her middle.

"You'll speak the same language," she said. "It's a baby, not a bird."

I nodded and left for the woods, pondering the wisdom of my wife. Fatherhood implies an automatic taming, the necessity of employment, a beginning of ownership. I'd expected glimmers of paternal anxiety but the onrush of fears was a box canyon ambush. I doubted my abilities to raise a child without ruining it. Although I trusted Rita implicitly, in my worst moments I worried that the baby might not be mine. At other times I was convinced that some long-buried Offutt gene would surface, producing a sideshow freak. Mainly, I was afraid that Rita's love would shift away from me.

Most of our friends were single and none had children. Some envied the pregnancy, while others considered us brave, possibly stupid. We had no one to talk to, no models of how people dealt with kids. I mentioned this in a pokergame, and a guy derisively asked if I thought I was the first man to father a child. I said nothing because the answer was yes, that was exactly how I felt. I knew that drastic change was coming, but had no way to prepare for it.

My life's progression had been a toxic voyage bringing me to the safety of the flatland, where I began each day by entering the woods along the river. I've become adept at tracking animals, finding the final footprint of skull and bone. Many people are afraid of the woods but that's where I keep my fears. I visit them every day. The trees know me, the riverbank accepts my path. Alone in the woods, it is I who is gestating, preparing for life.

Where I'm from, the foothills of southern Appalachia are humped like a kicked rug, full of steep furrows. Families live scattered among the ridges and hollows in tiny communities containing no formal elements save a post office. My hometown is a zip code with a creek. We used to have a store but the man who ran it died. Long before my birth, a union invalidated the company scrip, shut the mines, and left a few men dead. Two hundred people live there now.

Our hills are the most isolated area of America, the subject of countless doctoral theses. It's an odd sensation to read about yourself as counterpart to the aborigine or Eskimo. If VISTA wasn't bothering us, some clown was running around the hills with a tape recorder. Strangers told us we spoke Elizabethan English, that we were contemporary ancestors to everyone else. They told us the correct way to pronounce "Appalachia," as if we didn't know where we'd been living for the past three hundred years.

One social scientist proclaimed us criminal Scotch-Irish clansmen deemed unfit to live in Britain—our hills as precursor to Australia's penal colony. Another book called us the heirs to errant Phoenicians shipwrecked long before Columbus seduced Isabella for tub fare. My favorite legend made us Melungeons, a mysterious batch of folk possessing ungodly woodskills. We can spot fleas hopping from dog to dog at a hundred yards; we can track a week-old snake trail across bare rock. If you don't believe it, just ask the sociologist who spent a season like a fungus in the hills.

The popular view of Appalachia is a land where every man is willing, at the drop of a proverbial overall strap, to shoot, fight, or fuck anything on hind legs. We're men who buy half-pints of bootlegged liquor and throw the lids away in order to finish the whiskey in one laughing, brawling night, not caring where we wake or how far from home. Men alleged to eat spiders off the floor to display our strength, a downright ornery bunch.

The dirt truth is a hair different. The men of my generation live in the remnants of a world that still maintains a frontier mentality. Women accept and endure, holding the families tight. Mountain culture expects its males to undergo various rites of manhood, but genuine tribulation under fire no longer exists. We've had to create our own.

Once a week, Mom drove fifteen miles to town for groceries, accompanied by her children. We visited the interstate, which was creeping closer in tiny increments, bisecting hills and property, rerouting creeks. We called it the four-laner. It slithered in our direction like a giant snake. Mom said I-64 ran clear to California, a meaningless distance since none of us had ever crossed the county line. The completed road linked the world to the hills, but failed to connect us to the world.

I never intended to quit high school, but like many of my peers, I simply lost the habit. Education was for fools. Girls went to college seeking a husband; boys went to work. The pool hall's grimy floor, stained block walls, and furtive tension suited me well. The only requirement was adherence to an unspoken code of ethics, a complex paradigm that I still carry today. A rack of balls cost a dime, cheeseburgers a quarter. I ran the table three times in a row one day, and afterwards could not find a willing player. Inadvertently I had alienated myself from the only society that had ever tolerated me, a pattern that would continue for years.

After a week of shooting pool alone, I was ripe for an army recruiter who culled the pool hall like a pimp at Port Authority. I was under age but my parents gleefully signed the induction papers. The recruiter ferried me a hundred miles to Lexington, where I failed the physical examination.

"Albumin in the urine," the doctor said. "No branch will take you."

I felt weak. Tears cut lines down my face. My own body had trapped me in the hills, spirit pinioned by the flesh. I didn't know which was worse, the shame of physical betrayal or the humiliation of having cried in front of a hundred eager men-to-be. They moved away from me to hide their own embarrassment. I was subsequently denied admittance to the Peace Corps, park rangers, the ranks of firemen and police. I'd never know camaraderie, or test myself in sanctioned ways against other men.

That summer I began to steal and smoke dope, and in the fall I had no choice but to attend college. The only school within the mountains had recently become a university. After two years, I quit and announced my plans to become an actor in New York. Jennipher, the one girl I'd had the courage to love, had married a quarterback and moved far away. My sisters considered me a hopeless redneck. My brother refused to live with me, and my father and I hadn't spoken civilly in upwards of thirty-eight months.

Mom fixed me a sack lunch the morning I left. We sat quietly at the completed highway, staring at the fresh, clean blacktop. Mom was trying not to cry. I felt bad for being the first to erode the family, though I'd already been at it for a while. The road stretched to the horizon like a wide creek and I thought of Daniel Boone questing for space. The road in had become a way out.

Mom pressed a ten-dollar bill in my hand and dropped her head. "Write when you get work," she mumbled.

Birdsong spilled from the wooded hills. I began walking, the pack on my back angled like a cockeyed turtle shell. A pickup stopped and hauled me out of Kentucky. The hills relaxed their taut furls, billowing gently like sheets on a clothesline. I had a fresh haircut, two hundred dollars, and a grade school photograph of Jennipher. I was already homesick.

When I told drivers that I was heading for New York to be an actor, they grinned and shook their heads. A trucker pointed to the radio and told me to act like I was turning it on. I slept under a tree in Ohio and camped the next night behind a truck stop in Pennsylvania. On the third day, I entered the Holland Tunnel.

The world on the other side was so alien that my chief advantage was the ability to speak and read English. My accent's raucous twang betrayed me. I vowed to eliminate the guttural tones, swallowed endings, and stretching of single-syllable words. Until then, I remained silent. Manhattan was filthy and loud but similar to the hills: packed with illiterate men, unattainable women, and threat of injury. I regarded avenues as ridges, and the cross streets as hollows. Alleys were creeks that trickled into the river of Broadway. New York wasn't that big, just tall.

Like most groups of immigrants, Kentuckians abroad form a tight community that helps newcomers. Having left family and land, we could not quite rid ourselves of the clannish impulse dating back to the Celts. We still roved the civilized world, but no longer painted ourselves blue before the attack. I moved into an apartment on the Upper West Side with three natives of Kentucky. They were graduates of the college I'd quit, older students I vaguely knew, struggling actors. They let me sleep on the couch. The halls between apartments were so narrow that if two people met, both had to turn sideways for passage. More people lived in my building than on my home hill.

The city seemed predicated upon one's innate ability to wait, a learned craft, routine as tying a shoe. You had to wait for a buzzer to enter a building, wait for the subway, wait for an elevator. I stood for two hours in a movie line only to learn that it was sold out and the line was for the next showing, two more hours away. Groups of people rushed down subway steps, then stood perfectly still. They rushed onto the train, and again became immobile until their stop, whereupon they'd rush out. The waiting was more exhausting than motion. People hurried, I decided, not because they were late but because they were sick of standing still.

The simple act of walking became a problem for me. I kept bumping into people, often tripping them or myself. I'd never had this problem before, possessing if not grace, at least a certain agility and physical awareness. It seemed as if people rushed into my path. One Saturday I sat on a bench at midtown and watched pedestrians, seeking insight. My error was a long, steady stride, necessary to cover the open ground of home. I simply set myself in motion and put my legs to work. New Yorkers took quick, short steps. They darted and danced, stopped short and sidestepped, constantly twisting their torsos and dipping their shoulders to dodge people. Since everyone was likewise engaged, the whole comedic street dance worked. I took a bus home and practiced in my room. As long as I concentrated, everything was jake, but the minute my attention wavered, my gait lengthened and someone's legs entangled with mine.

I spent another two hours observing foot traffic and noticed that most New Yorkers possessed a morbid fear of automobiles. They assiduously avoided the curb, which left a narrow open lane at the edge of the sidewalk. I began walking as close to the gutter as possible.

My roommates were seldom home. To show appreciation for having been taken in, I decided to wash everyone's laundry. The laundromat was a narrow chamber, very hot. I was the only white person and the only male. Conversation around me was incomprehensible. I'd read about black dialects of the inner city and was pleased in an odd way that I couldn't understand what was being said. English had been melted and recast into their own tongue. It reminded me of being home. I wanted to tell the women that my native language was equally enigmatic to outsiders.

Folding laundry was a skill I lacked, and I started with the sheets, believing them to be easier. My arms weren't long enough to span the sheet and it dragged the floor. I tried to fold it like a flag, draping one end over the table and working forward. The table didn't provide enough tension and again the sheet slipped to the floor. I sorted a few socks while considering the problem.

Controlling the four corners of the sheet was essential, which led to a plan of theoretic elegance. I doubled the sheet and held two of its corners. I spread my legs, mentally counted to three, and threw the sheet into the air, snapping my wrists. The sheet unfurled and arced back. I caught one corner but missed the other. Encouraged, I took a deep breath and concentrated, knowing that I needed a slight correction in toss and grab. As I threw the sheet, someone entered the laundromat, producing a strong draft. The sheet blew over my head and shoulders. I dropped one corner. Unable to see, I stepped forward, placed my foot on the sheet and not so much fell as actually pulled myself to my knees. I jerked the sheet off my head. Above the cacophony of washers and dryers came the pearly sound of women laughing.

They walked past me and started folding my laundry. Perfect columns of T-shirts began to rise on the table. With an unerring sense of size, the women sorted the pants into stacks corresponding to my roommates and me. They refused my assistance and talked among themselves. I listened carefully, trying to isolate a word or phrase, but they spoke too fast for me to follow. They moved to their own chores without looking at me, as if embarrassed by their benevolence. I approached the nearest woman and thanked her. She nodded.

"I'm from Kentucky," I said. "It's not like New York."

"Nothing is."

"How did you learn to fold clothes so well?"

"My mother taught me."

"In Harlem?"

Her eyes widened and her lips drew tight across her teeth. I realized the stupidity of assuming that all blacks grew up in Harlem, like thinking all Kentuckians came from Lexington or Louisville. She bent to her work, her face furious.

"I'm sorry," I said. "Maybe not Harlem."

"No! Not Harlem."

"Where, then?"

"Puerto Rico. I am Puerto Rico!" She lifted her arms to include everyone in the laundromat. "Puerto Rico!"

"Puerto Rico," I said.

"*Sí.*"

I leaned against the table, absolutely clobbered by an awareness that they'd been speaking Spanish. During the next few days, I wandered the blocks near my building. It was not a black neighborhood as I'd previously thought. Everyone was of Hispanic descent, but I felt more comfortable here than among the white people. My culture had much in common with the Latin—loyalty to a family that was often large, respect for the elderly and for children, a sharp delineation between genders. The men were governed by a sense of machismo similar to that which ruled in the hills. There was one quite obvious drawback—to them I was just another white man.

The random progress of a nose-down dog dropped me into a job on the Lower East Side of Manhattan. Belched from the subway each morning, I strolled the Bowery past dozens of men dirty as miners. Many could not speak. Each payday, I gave away two packs' worth of cigarettes, one at a time.

For six months I worked at a warehouse in the neighborhood, the first full-time job of my life. I collected clothing orders for a professional shipping clerk with forty years' experience. His passive numbness frightened me. I was a gatherer of shirts and slacks; he was a hunter of numbers. The day's highlight was staring at a Polaroid of a nude woman I'd found on the street. Ancient priests of South America used fake knives and animal blood to save the sacrificial virgins for themselves. Up north I just wanted a goddess to worship.

After work, I saw a tall woman with a huge jaw being harassed by a junkie. I chased the junkie away. The woman smiled and led me to an abandoned subway station with a boarded entrance. A pink dress hung loose on her lanky frame. She pried three planks free and slipped in, motioning down the steps to a bare mattress. She wasn't attractive, but no one else had shown me the least bit of attention. I followed her. A musty breeze from the bowels of the earth fluttered trash along the floor. I felt snug and primal in the dank urban temple. I would become an albino, a blind white harlot in service to Ishtar.

She asked for a match. When I lit her cigarette, she caressed my face and grabbed my crotch, lashing my tongue with hers. I slid my hand down her stomach and between her legs. My fingers hit something hard tucked low against her abdomen. I was accustomed to people carrying guns and it seemed natural for a woman alone in the city to be armed. The only feasible option was to gain control of the pistol.

I ran my hand up her dress, wrapped my fingers around the barrel, and gave a quick tug. She moaned low and very deep. I pulled again and suddenly realized the gun was made of flesh. My entire body trembled in a fury of incomprehension. I stood, unable to speak. She threw her purse at me and laughed a taunting cackle that echoed in the tunnel. I ran up the stairs, plunged through the opening, and fell on the sidewalk. Two men holding hands stepped off the curb to avoid me.

The following day, I called in sick to the warehouse and stayed in the tub all day. When the water cooled, I refilled it, still hearing that laughter throbbing in my head. I was sure I'd found a circus freak, a hermaphrodite, the only one in the city and perhaps the entire country. At nineteen, it was beyond my understanding that a grown man would impersonate a female. Not all transvestites are gay, I later learned, but mine was. This seemed a crucial difference between the city and the hills—Appalachian men could acceptably fornicate with daughters, sisters, and livestock, but carnal knowledge of a man was a hanging offense.

I ate lunch daily at a diner on Great Jones Street. The joint was a showcase of deformity—goiters swelled throats, and tumors jutted from bodies, stretching gray skin. Hair sprouted in odd places. The owner kept a sawed-off shotgun close at hand. One day a stray woman appeared in a booth. She was short and dark, wearing tight pants which I studied closely for a telltale bulge. She noticed my observation and I quickly looked away. She moved near.

"Are you a mechanic?" she said. "My car needs work."

"No. I'm an actor. Are you a girl?"

"Everybody I know is bisexual now."

"Not me," I said. "Want to go to the museum on Saturday?"

"Can't."

"Why not?"

"Just can't. Why don't you visit me in Brooklyn on Sunday."

"Where's Brooklyn?"

She laughed and spoke loudly to all. "He wants to know where Brooklyn is!"

The simple purity of Jahi's directions enthralled me: Take the Flatbush train to the end and get out. Walk down the street and go left. Ring the second bell. Finding a place at home involved landmarks such as the creek, the big tree, or the third hollow past the wide place in the road. After the quantum mechanics of lower Manhattan, Brooklyn sounded like simple geometry. I bought a new shirt for the date. That she was black didn't matter—she was female and I was lonely. We were both at the bottom of our republic's fabled melting pot.

Noisy people thronged the streets of Flatbush Avenue. Tattoos covered the men like subway graffiti. Women wore neon skirts drawn so tight that their thighs brushed audibly at every step. The stores were barred by padlocked gates that reminded me of ramparts under siege.

Jahi's apartment was absolutely bare save for a couch, a table, two chairs, and a bed. We drank wine and passed a joint. After four hours she seduced me because, she later told me, I had not pounced on her all afternoon. She considered me a southern gentleman. I didn't mention the white trash truth—every country boy knew city women would breed quicker than a striking snake. Expecting sex as urban custom, I was in no hurry. Plus I didn't know much about it.

When the time came, I pounded into her, spurted, and rolled away. She raised her eyebrows and blinked several times.

"Are you a virgin?" she said.

"How could I be?"

"You don't have to use your whole body. Just your hips."

"I know," I said quickly.

"Look, nobody knows until they learn."

"I've read about it plenty."

"I'm not saying anything against you, Chris. Everybody's different and you may as well learn about me."

She stood on the bed and told me to look at her body very carefully. I'd never seen a woman fully nude before. Jahi had a peculiar frame—strongly muscled dancer's legs, a delightful bottom, and the dark torso of a young girl. Her small breasts sported enormous nipples, ebon pegs an inch long, hard as clay. A few black hairs surrounded them, reminding me of crippled spiders.

She lay beside me and invited me to touch her everywhere, methodic as a surveyor, covering every square inch. Next she explained the complex labyrinth of her plumbing. From its nook she retrieved her clitoris and demonstrated the proper action for maximum pleasure. She counseled me on the rising barometer of orgasm and cued me to a steady drilling until the dam broke. I received a cursory lecture on the soft crest where buttock met leg, the inner thigh, and lastly the anus. I balked, believing this too advanced. With time, she assured me, even that arena would be old hat.

Two hours later I was a sweaty scholar eager to matriculate. Jahi rolled on her back and aimed her heels at the ceiling while I wriggled down the graduation aisle. Propping my weight on knees and elbows allowed her some maneuvering room. The prescribed circular motion reminded me of sharpening a knife on an oily whetstone: apply pressure on the upstroke and ease away, alternating sides for a balanced edge.

To forestall ejaculation, she had suggested I concentrate on baseball. I thought about Cincinnati's Big Red Machine, squirmed my hips correctly, and remembered how the manager always hopped over the sprinkled white baseline to avoid bad luck. The summer I turned twelve, VISTA bused a load of hill boys to Crosley Field for a game. In the parking lot I was astounded to see a black kid, the first I'd ever seen. He was my size and wore clothes identical to mine—jeans and T-shirt. I stared at him so hard that I walked into a streetlight, which didn't exist in the hills either. The VISTA man made me sit beside him the whole game.

Suddenly Jahi was squirming like an epileptic, thrashing her legs and ripping my back. Convinced I'd made a mistake, I slowed the rhythm to a bullpen warm-up. The manager's hand signals blurred to gibberish and she began screaming.

"Fuck me, you white motherfucker!"

Appalled, I pistoned my hips until the dugout began moving across the floor. I went to my fastball right down the old piperino. Hum, baby, hum. I fiddled and diddled, kicked and delivered.

"Give it to me," she grunted.

"I am, I am!"

"Talk dirty."

"What?"

"Talk dirty!"

"Well, hell," I said. "You're a horse's ass."

She clicked into automatic pilot, writhing and moaning, cursing and shrieking. "You like this!" she bellowed. "You like fucking me!"

I loosened my tongue for locker room talk. "Batter up, batter down, who's that monkey on the mound?"

"I'm coming!"

"She's coming around third. Here's the throw. It's in the dirt, safe at home!"

My body twitched, heat surging from my feet and skull to join at the crotch and erupt. The fans shrieked my name. They were leaping from the stands, peeling the artificial turf, ripping bases out of the ground. Pooled sweat like celebration champagne swirled down my side as I rolled over.

"That was great, Jahi!"

"Yeah, you're a natural."

She gave me a postgame pep talk on how to talk dirty in bed. I nodded and thanked her and she sent me out for pizza, her scent covering me like infield dust. I relived the game in my mind, conjuring instant replays of the best parts.

During the next few weeks, Jahi commandeered my urban safari to Coney Island, Times Square, Radio City, and a hundred bars in between. On the Staten Island Ferry she climbed over the railing to dangle by her arms. The murky water whirlpooled below, filled with plastic tampon tubes and toxic fish. Jahi grinned at me and kicked the side of the boat.

"Don't jump," she yelled. "Hang on, Chris. Hang on!"

After the crew hauled her up, she began hurling life preservers overboard. "I can't swim," she explained. "I have to save myself."

The angry captain assigned us a guard, whom Jahi charmed through subtle exposure of her chest. He leaned to the port for a glimpse down her shirt. The boat rocked in the wake of a tug and he stumbled, face red, and banned her from the ferry.

"Starting when?" she said.

"Now."

"Stop the boat!" she yelled. "Take me back." She slapped him across the face. "That nutball grabbed my ass. Help, help!"

Passengers turned away in a slack-eyed city manner, but a couple of burly men advanced. Jahi grabbed them by their belt buckles, one in each tiny hand.

"He's the one," she said, her voice sliding into the plaintive tone of a child. "He's the one who touched me down there."

One of her saviors had two tears tattooed below his right eye. At the base of his hairline were the letters H.A.N.Y.C. The taller one had a subway token embedded in his ear hole, the flesh grown around it like a board nailed to a tree.

"Which one," the tall guy said.

"Don't know," Jahi said. "Can't remember."

"Stomp both," said the other one.

"It was him." The boat guard pointed at me. "He's the freak."

"Rat knows its own hole," the tall one said.

"Yeah," I said. "Smeller's the feller."

The hard guys looked at me and I realized that I'd pulled their focus from the uniform.

"You two are big bullies," Jahi said.

She spread her legs and arched her back, tipping her head to look up at them. Her voice came hard and mean.

"Nervous without your hogs. I'd half-and-half you on the spot if you took a shower. Don't dime me on this fucking tub, boys. Here's the front. The citizen's with me but he's cherry for a mule. The boat heat's a cowboy looking for a notch. You clippers cross the wise and it's a hard down, with no help from your brothers. They took their taste last night in the Alphabet."

The bikers stiffened beneath her onslaught, eyes turning reptile-flat. The tall one eased backwards, disappearing among the passengers, his friend following. The boat guard tracked them at a coward's distance. Jahi wiped a sheen of sweat from each temple.

"What was all that?" I asked. "I didn't understand a word you said."

"They did." She brushed her knuckles against my crotch. "You understand this, right?"

I nodded and when the ferry docked across the bay, we crawled into one of the emergency rowboats lashed to the side and frolicked in the bow.

The following Saturday she took me to the nude area of Rockaway Beach, where fat voyeurs trailed ugly women. Men with perfect hair trooped naked in pairs. I remembered my grandmother's opinion of a *Playgirl* magazine my sister showed her one Christmas. "They're just like on the farm," Grandmaw had said. "All those old-fashioned pumps with the handles hanging down."

Jahi chose a few square yards of dirty sand amid condoms and cigarette butts. I've always hated the beach except in winter. The sun's too hot, the sea's too cold, and the presence of humanity spoils any natural beauty still lurking in the sand. Jahi refused to disrobe on the grounds that she was brown enough. We'd never discussed her heritage and I didn't want to embarrass myself with the stupidity of asking if she tanned. She insisted that I undress. Since I would not lie on my stomach and proffer myself to the steady parade of men, I lay on my back. The sun scorched my testicles within five minutes.

Jahi teased me for days. In the subway she cocked her head, voice loud to draw attention.

"Are your balls still sunburnt, Chris? They must itch like fire." She addressed the nearest stranger. "Burnt to cinders at the beach. If he's not bragging, he's complaining."

Our public time was a constant duel designed to make me angry, jealous, or embarrassed. As she ran low on ammo against my nonchalance, her improvisations became more outrageous. While waiting for a train, she asked a stranger's opinion of my eyes. Soon she had him leaning close to inspect my face. He agreed that my eyes were slightly crossed, especially the left one. "Yes," she said. "That one has got to go. Do you have a knife? You take it out. You, you, you!"

We rode the subway for hours per day, Jahi's method of rehearsing for her stage career with myriad strangers as her audience. She considered her antics a necessary corrective to my rural background. In the middle of mischief, she'd grin my way, eager for approval. She once stole a ream of paper and opened the bundle on a windy sidewalk. "Oh my God!" she shrieked. "My manuscript!" We watched twelve samaritans chase blank pages down the avenue. At a topless bar she removed her shirt to bus tables, piling empty glasses on the lap of a drunk who'd been pawing the dancers. A bouncer with shoulders like a picnic table came our way. I stayed in my chair, aware that standing would get my head thumped, trusting Jahi to avert trouble.

"Hey, sugar," the bouncer said to her. "You need a job? We could use your kind of spunk."

"I got a job," she said, pointing to me. "I watch out for him. He's a famous actor."

The bouncer helped Jahi with her coat, then turned to me. "You're a lucky man, my friend."

That evening we lounged in her apartment while twilight pollution streaked orange across the sky. Construction noise had ceased at the nearby condo site where future dwellers would pay extra for the fetid river breeze. Jahi had spent the day trying unsuccessfully to make me jealous on the street. Angry at herself, she told me my acting career was a joke. I spent too much time merely watching, writing in my journal.

I'd never told her about my single audition, crammed into a hot room with sixty guys, each of whom clutched a satchel of résumés. Everyone seemed to know each other, like members of a club. They sparred and parried in dirty verbal fighting until a slow response brought on a death jab. The winner smiled and wished the loser luck.

When my name was called, I stepped through a door and crossed the dark stage to an oval swatch of light. Someone thrust a typed page into my hand. A nasal voice whined from the darkness: "Start at the red arrow."

Twenty seconds later the same voice interrupted to thank me. Confused, I nodded and continued reading.

"I said thank you," the voice said. "Can someone please . . ."

A hand took my arm while another retrieved the script. They led me away like an entry at the county fair, a recalcitrant steer who'd balked before the judging stand. I decided to become a movie actor, and skip fooling around with the legitimate theater.

Jahi had surreptitiously removed her underwear from beneath her dress. The thin cloth dangled from her foot. She kicked and her panties arched neatly onto my head.

"Do you write about me?" she said.

"Maybe."

"You should."

"Why?"

"Because I'm alive."

"So am I, Jahi."

"Without me, you weren't. You were young, dumb, and full of come. Now you're just young."

"I'm glad you don't think I'm dumb anymore."

"Oh you are, Chris. I made you smart enough to know you are, that's all. Write that in your little notebook."

The journal was my combat arena, the final refuge of privacy in a city of eight million. Each day I saw perhaps two thousand different faces, an enjoyable fact until I realized that my face was one of the two thousand each of them saw too. My math collapsed from the exponential strain. Jahi wasn't in my journal. Those pages were filled with me. Some of the pages held my full name and place of birth on every line to remind me that I lived.

"Write down everything I say," she said. "Make me live forever."

"Come on, Jahi. I don't even write good letters."

"You don't know it but you will. You'll reach a point where you have no choice."

"Yeah, and I can be president too."

"You can do anything you want. You're a white American man."

"Right."

"And I'm a nigger bitch who sleeps with Whitey."

"Goddamn it, Jahi!"

"See," she muttered through a smile. "I knew I could get to you."

I stomped the floor. "I don't care what you pull on the street. Go naked! Start trouble! You're the only friend I've got, remember. There's maybe fifty people who know me at home. Everybody in Brooklyn knows you, and half of Manhattan. I'm the nobody, not you!"

"Not forever." Her voice dulled to a monotone, "I traveled your dreams."

She stiffened to catatonia, eyes glazed, her fingers twined in her lap. She tensed her jaw to stop the chattering of her teeth.

"You will make gold from lead, flowers from ash. Cut the scabs and stab them. Cut the scabs—"

"Stop it, Jahi."

I considered slapping her, but had never hit a female and wasn't sure if it was different from hitting a man. Her droning halted before I found out. Jahi slid from the couch to the floor, limbs pliant as rope. The pulse in her neck throbbed very fast. She opened her eyes and rubbed her face with the back of her fists, looking around as if lost.

"Has that happened before?" I said.

"Many times," she said. "You never asked about my family."

"So what. You didn't ask about mine."

She moved across the floor to my feet, gently stroking my leg. Her eyes were very old. I noticed gray in her hair.

"I didn't know my father," she said. "My mother was an Obeah woman from the mountains. She died before I learned to control what she taught. I went to Kingston and hustled money. I came to Brooklyn when I was sixteen, too old for work down there. I can't help what I am."

"What?"

"They said I was a witch bastard whore in Jamaica. Here they just say I'm crazy."

She sighed and tipped her face to mine.

"I feel the new gray hair," she said. "Pluck it."

I obeyed. She flicked it with her fingers and the hair whipped, taut as wire.

"Strong," she muttered. "I see strong tonight."

She leaned against my legs and closed her eyes. Through the window and over the tenement roofs, the full moon gleamed like the top of a skull. No doubt she was a tad nutty, but I hadn't met anyone in the city who wasn't. New York appeared to be a voluntary asylum where all the cranks and sociopaths escaped from their small towns; nobody I knew had been born and raised there. Half the population was crazy and the rest were therapists.

The moon disappeared into the neon glare. Jahi faded into sleep. I moved to the couch and opened my journal. It had begun as proof of my identity, but under Jahi's onslaught, it began a transformation as I tentatively set my goal to be an actual writer. The standard rule was to write what you know, but I did not believe I knew anything worthwhile. The only thing I could write with any confidence was a considered record of daily events.

Jahi found me on the couch, fully clothed. She was giddy with a plan to ride horses the following Saturday. When the unicorn came for her, she wanted to be ready. I bragged outrageously at my ability to ride. After two months of tagging behind her in the city, I was eager for a familiar undertaking.

We rode the train to Prospect Park. Jahi wore a pair of brand-new jodhpurs given to her by her sugar daddy, a phrase I didn't understand. We found a bunch of kids on ancient mares with cracked saddles. The guy in charge was a weight lifter named Tony, dressed in boots, Stetson, and fringed shirt. When I asked where he was from, he said, "Roun' de co'nuh."

Tony led his motley posse along a dirt path through the park. The horses walked a lazy single file. Half an hour later they still strolled with heads down, performing their function like machines. I was embarrassed for the animals, domesticated to disgrace.

Tony left the path for a wide paved road that curved around a pond. The horses began a brief trot. Following instinct, I snapped the reins across the horse's neck and hunkered down. A gallop was much easier to ride. The old mare lifted her head and, for the first time since retiring to Brooklyn, heaved into a run. Her hooves sounded odd pounding the tar. I guided her to the outside and around the others. Jahi whooped behind me.

Tony shouted for me to stop, his face red and snarling, finally looking as if he was from the neighborhood instead of Montana. I floated above the pavement, well seated and moving with the mare's rhythm. I looked for Jahi and saw a horse following at full speed. Someone screamed. I reined in and a horse shot past me, its rider slowly tilting sideways like a centaur splitting at the seam. The horse swerved toward the edge of the road. The rider slid from the saddle. His head slammed against a streetlight, spinning his body in a pinwheel, slinging blood that spattered the street.

A few hundred people formed a tight circle around the kid. Teen-age boys dared each other to step in the blood. An ambulance arrived. Tony was mad and wanted to fight but Jahi pulled me away, screaming that she'd sue. She held very tightly to my arm, pushing her groin against my leg. Her palms were hot.

We took a cab to her apartment. She hurried upstairs and when I walked in, she was waiting, bent over the back of the couch with the jodhpurs at her ankles.

"Please, Chris," begged her disembodied voice.

Mechanically I unbuckled my pants. As I lowered them, I heard again the sound of the boy's head hitting the steel pole, like a boot dropped into a fifty-gallon drum. Swallowing bile, I turned and ran down the steps. The public sacrifice had been too great, too unex-pected. I was unable to merge with the priestess for recovery of life.

I wandered Flatbush in a muddled stupor. The day's event un-furled in my head at varying speeds. I watched the scene from above in slow motion, seeing myself on a tiny horse. I became the kid sliding for miles from the saddle, waiting for impact. I became Tony, drop-jawed and aghast, primed for a fight. I was the horse; I was Jahi; I was the bored medic. I was anyone but myself.

I missed work for a week, staying in bed like a hog wrapped in the warm, wet mud of misery. When I finally went to the warehouse, Jahi called, petulant and forgiving. I hung up on her laughter and never saw her again.

A week later, on my twentieth birthday, I joined some guys play-ing football in Riverside Park. Quick and lean with good hands, I made a spectacular catch on a thirty-yard pass. The ball was spi-raling high, thrown too hard and over my head. I leaped, twisting in the air to snag it from the sky, seeing at my zenith the New Jersey smokestacks reflected in the river's glare. My left foot landed one way while my momentum carried me the other. A tackler smashed me a third direction altogether.

The next day I limped to a hospital and emerged with my left leg encased in plaster. The knee ligaments were destroyed but I was happy. The cast gave me a legitimate reason for going home. I rode an airplane for the first time and my mother picked me up in Lexington. She drove me two hours into the eastern hills, where the community accepted my return as a wounded hero. My family's attitude was one of justice having been done; the cosmos had exacted its price for the sheer audacity of leaving the land. Dad and I drank beer together, a rite we'd never performed before. He repeated again and again, "They shoot horses in your shape."

The cast was due for removal in eight weeks but took ten because the local doctor had to import a special cutting tool. He was so impressed with the New York cast that he asked to keep it. My leg revealed itself pale, withered, and hairless. Every evening, I filled a purse with rocks, fastened it to my ankle, and lifted it from a sitting position. Between repetitions I plucked ticks from the dogs, watching night arrive. The black air seeped down the hills to fuse land and sky in a darkness absent from the city.

My acting career had failed but I had been to all the museums, and many galleries. The paintings overpowered me. I often sat for hours before a single canvas, studying each nuance of brushstroke, seeking to understand not the painting, but the painter. Galleries had the effect of a swift cold shower. Museums left me exhausted. Limping in the womb of the hills, I decided to become a painter without ever having applied brush to canvas. First, I needed a job to finance the supplies. Second, I needed unusual clothes. Third and most important, I needed inspiration.

I thought of Jahi offering herself as reward for violence. I had shunned the ritual as a petrifact. Becoming a grownup had to mean

more than sex, needed to be independent of women. The traditional
arena of sports had left me with a leg unable to tolerate the required
pivots. I could stay at home and cut trees, dig the earth, and kill
animals, but using nature as my testing ground would prove nothing. The woods were full of damaged men. Nature always won.

Willows are budding along the river, and young birds already sing from the nest. Rita's had an easy first couple of months. She sleeps late, takes a daily nap, and has vomited only once. Until then, we were afraid that since she'd had no morning sickness, there might be something wrong. I was proud of her mess.

Lately she has begun traipsing from the closet to the mirror.

"Do I look pregnant?" she asks.

"No," I say, believing that she's trying to hide her weight. She curls on the bed and cries. I join her, stroking her hair, slowly realizing that she's been choosing clothes to emphasize her belly, not conceal it. Rita wants everyone to know. Since becoming pregnant, she leans her shoulders back and rubs her stomach, resembling someone who just ate a fine meal, instead of a woman carrying a child. Now she's finally showing.

Barring outright violence, the worst move a man can make is abandoning a pregnant woman. The act, however, is not uncommon. I now understand the motivation as uncontrollable fear, rather than desire for freedom or a different mate. Male terror looms in tandem with the woman's rising belly. She is changing; he is not. Her body and mind drastically alter day by day while he's still the knucklehead he always was.

The prospect of spending a life with Rita impels a scrutiny of her smallest traits that aggravate me like saddle burrs. In the woods I speculate on which habit will drive me to mania at age sixty—not screwing the lid on a ketchup bottle hard enough, or leaving her clothes scattered like pollen about the house. She would prefer that I answer the phone politely and change my clothes more often. The compromise of pair bonding is the acceptance of previously unacceptable personal traits.

In Kentucky there are two clubs for young boys—4-H and Future Farmers of America. I joined both for the field trips, one of which was to the state fair. We were bused two hundred miles to the grounds—a vast spectacle, bigger than the nearest town in the hills. One exhibit was of a live cow with a plexiglas window in its side. The hide had been peeled back, the flesh removed, and I could watch the churning of its digestive system, the regurgitation and movement of food from one stomach to another. It turned me against milk for a year.

If I could somehow see inside Rita, I'd feel less uneasy about the baby. The library books say it's an embryo until the eighth week, when all the organs are formed. At that point it's a fetus the size of a thumb. Photographs make me think of a tiny whale, its heart directly behind the mouth, an eating machine. There is no peephole to Rita's belly but I have to accept that a baby's in there. As with God or black holes, one goes by the surrounding evidence.

Yesterday the county Civil Defense warned us of impending flood. They offered free sand, but we'd have to fill the bags ourselves. I drank coffee all night, crossing the yard with a flashlight every half hour. The water rose faster than Rita's belly. I held tightly to a post, as if the river might suck me into its current. I imagined Rita and me in the boat, the typewriter and child between us, hunting a knoll. Trees crashed into the river, the soil of their roots eaten away by the swiftly rising water. The storm continued through the night.

At dawn today the river's dark surface runs thick as milk. It has crested two feet from our bank. A single goose sits fifty yards away, black-necked with a white patch on his throat like a chin strap to a lost helmet. It hasn't moved in two hours. Lightning has sheared a branch from a tree, and the trunk is scarred by the burn. Siberian shamans made sacred drums from such trees, but this one isn't fresh enough. After twelve hours, the electricity's power has faded. Beneath its overhang a great blue heron breaks from shore, long neck tucked in a curl, wings lifting slowly like a prehistoric bird. A bloated cow floats by, eyeholes pecked to vacancy by crows.

The anchor for my boat is a coffee can filled with cement. The rope is too short for the sudden rise of water. It holds the bow below the surface, the anchor line a false umbilicus. The motor rides high in the back while the gas tank drifts between seats. The boat is filled with river. All the life jackets have floated away.

A line of geese flies downriver, shifting direction as a group, following the telepathy of flight. Ravens can be taught to copy human speech, and I suppose if my tongue were split, I could talk with birds. They would impart the secrets of their hollow bones, and I could tell them how lucky they were to limit reproduction to eggs. An outbuilding is drifting by, a wooden shed built too near the bank for safety. A squirrel crouches on the ridgepole. A coil of wire still hangs from a nail.

Rita is at work. She dropped me off at home after our monthly checkup. We feel lucky to have our doctor; she is honest and forthright. It is like visiting a favorite sister. She allows me to peek over her shoulder when shining a flashlight deep into Rita's innards. Everything's red in there. I don't know what I'm seeing and don't want to ask. After the exam, the doctor says Rita has an "easy uterus." If a man had said that, I might have been offended.

She smeared grease on Rita's belly and pressed a microphone left of her navel. A cord ran to a small speaker. We listened to the fetal heartbeat miked in the tiny room. The baby had a quick rhythm that harmonized with Rita's slower pulse. I asked if we could turn off the lights and listen. Rita nodded to the doctor; they allow me little moments, slight involvements. The twining sounds of heartbeat reminded me of the night of the storm. The baby is rain. Rita is the steady gush of river. I am alone in the dark on the bank.

In the aftermath of flood, the river hurts like a man's blood when his brother dies. Plastic trash hangs in tree limbs to mark the water's crest. Beavers are chewing high on the trees, and after the waters recede, there will be evidence to suggest giant beavers—the tapered marks of their teeth far above my head. I have a need to believe in giants because the real ones are gone: three-toed sloths, the buffalo, soon the elephant. During flood, young beavers can drown in their hutch, trapped by the flow. Rita's body is heavy with fluid. There can be no sandbagging against a child, no evacuation, no warning of miscarriage.

A picnic table from town floats upside down near my bank. I tie a brick to a rope and chase the table a half mile before lassoing it on a lucky shot. I loop the rope around a tree. When the flood goes away, I'll drag the table into our yard. We'll have picnics and carve our names into the wood. I am practicing for the role of provider. My boots are scuffed and muddy.

The current is slower in the space just after a bend, and I watch a brave cormorant trying to fish there. Its skinny neck pokes from the surface like a snake. They migrate twice yearly and this one must have gotten lost in the storm, separated from its flock. Cormorants lack the waterproofing oil of ducks, thus are able to swim underwater, hunting fish. A thousand years of this has given them huge webbed feet set far enough back on the body to act as flippers. This makes them top-heavy. When a cormorant tries to walk on land, it falls to its chest like a dog on ice.

I feel a similar awkwardness now, unsure of what I've done, what I must later do. I'm not afraid of aging but of how the aged are supposed to behave. Science claims that human superiority is the result of a prolonged infancy and childhood; it seems more like luck to me. The cormorant can swim and fly, like the baby in Rita's womb. I am stuck with common walking. This flood is nothing compared with the coming deluge.

A ruined canoe has jammed itself into the riverbank, rearing like a tombstone marking the future of the past. Its dark, shiny bow reminds me of the dolphins who attempted dry terrain eons back. They slid onto the sun-warmed rocks and stayed long enough to lose their gills and miss the sea. Many dolphins fled to safety, but an outpost remained. They slowly became earless seals, marooned forever at the edge of dirt and water. I wonder if fatherhood will be the same.

I left Kentucky as soon as the doctor pronounced me healed, a diagnosis only physically correct. I roamed the country on foot, finding day labor and cheap rooms. I was a perpetual new face, the truck stop beggar, the sleeper on a bench, a tired battered bum not quite twenty-one. Each time my life became simple, a boss offered a promotion, or a woman wanted love. Fearing a trap, I grabbed my pack and left another life behind, heading like Daniel Boone for elbow room.

I moved vaguely through America and picked up a few more jobs—moving furniture, picking fruit, tarring a roof, driving a truck—all of which I despised. The effort of labor reminded me of a hangover. If you can only get through the next few hours, both come to an end. The tough part is accepting the wait until you can eat and drink again.

In autumn, a trucker left me in Minneapolis, a city as cold as a crowbar. At the employment office a young Chippewa offered me a place to stay. Marduk led me through glass tubes suspended over the city into a neighborhood of rickety buildings instead of the bison hide tipis I expected. Smoke signals emanated from the St. Paul factories across the river.

Daniel Boone had left civilization for a simpler life, killed his first buffalo in Kentucky, and was captured by the Shawnee. He took the name Sheltowee, which meant "Big Turtle." Boone's rite of adoption involved the careful plucking of hair to leave a scalplock. He was then stripped and scrubbed raw at a river to take his white blood out. My friendship with Marduk began on easier footing.

He was my age, trapped between rebellion against the traditions of his people and a hatred for Scandinavian whites. He told me there were more unearthed Indians in museums than were alive in the country. His great-grandmother was on display in Chicago. Marduk's father owned a car wash and wanted him for a partner; his mother was a powwow dancer, active in tribal rights. Marduk had no interest in either way of life. He wanted someday to enter the South American jungle and be a "real Indian." Pinched hard by both ends of his own culture, he lived among the city's newest immigrant group, the Hispanics.

Our roommates were twin brothers from Ecuador who considered Kentucky another country. We were all foreigners in the land of the free. When we drank rum, Marduk locked himself in his room to smoke dope, shouting through the door, "I will not be a drunken Indian!"

Luis and Javier were rare men who had actually achieved their childhood dream—employment as small-time gangsters. They lived better than they had at home. By North American standards, we were all poor as dirt, but the brothers desired no more than the life of a quiet desperado—a quality I envied. My ambitions were vague as mist. I spent most of my days at the museum, studying the edges of canvases, pleased to find sloppy craftsmanship. I filled my journal with opinions on art. My eventual work would show the world what was wrong with contemporary painting.

At night the three of us plunged into the icy streets, wind scything our legs and watering our eyes. We hurried from bar to bar, delivering illegal punchboards and occasionally the prize money. My presence helped when dealing with white bartenders. Given to bravado, Luis and Javier told me extravagant lies about our activities, but their tense silence informed me when we were transferring large sums. If they entered a back room, I was posted near the door as lookout. They never advised me on what to do in case of trouble.

A special mission sent us to an empty bar with few tables, more of a private club than a working saloon. The boys were delivering a payoff for the crooked punchboards, a fixed payoff in fact, a reward for someone who'd been told what number to choose, at which bar, on the specific day. It was the return of a favor. We were part of a string of cutout men, thereby making the money impossible to track.

A cop walked in and asked me where the bartender was. I shrugged, hoping the dim light would prevent his noticing the outbreak of sweat on my forehead. I began to wonder what form Luis and Javier's retribution would take if I failed to warn them.

"I'm homesick for Kentucky, buddy," I said. "Help me on the chorus, will you."

I began singing "My Old Kentucky Home," loud and out of tune. The bartender hurried from the back room. The cop raised his eyebrows at me, and the bartender tapped his temple while rolling his eyes. The cop nodded. I continued to sing. The bartender passed a thick envelope to the cop, who left.

Luis and Javier were very proud of my behavior and promised to recommend me to the boss. The bartender set us up with round after round, and by evening's end, we had sung "My Old Kentucky Home" so many times that the regulars had either joined in or left for a quieter place.

We stumbled home, where the brothers found Marduk asleep in a full bathtub with a one-hit bong on the floor. They hurried to my room, whispering demands that I come and see. When I refused, they became belligerent and dragged me to the bathroom. Marduk's arms hung over the sides of the tub. His head was tipped against the back rim. Floating between his legs was the largest lingam I'd ever seen. I stared with awe, remembering that only one tenth of an iceberg is visible above the water line. Javier flicked an empty toilet paper roll into the tub. Marduk's lingam drifted like a whale in the riffle, dwarfing the cardboard tube.

Luis whispered that Marduk had never known a woman. Twice he'd tried, with disastrous results that sent the females running in fear. The twins shook their heads in disappointment over the Wasted Monster, as they called it.

"Women are lucky," said Luis, "the Indian has the Monster and not me. They would not be safe if it was mine."

"You would be killed," answered Javier. "A husband would shoot you and cut the Monster off."

"The women would cry for a week."

"For two weeks."

"A month!"

A few nights later they collected fifty-five dollars from their fellow grifters and hoods against the size of Marduk's genitals. I held the money, not because they trusted me but as the mascot white boy I knew better than to make tracks with the booty. Daniel Boone the honest Quaker was proving his trust. Eight of us marched through snow to our third-floor dump, where the bettors ranged the living room like a guerrilla force.

I knocked at Marduk's door and walked in. He was asleep on his stomach.

"Wake up," I said. "You have to meet some people."

"Mm-uhmmm."

I shook his shoulder but a night's worth of marijuana had sedated him. I announced that Marduk was deep in his dope sleep and nothing would wake him. Luis and Javier glanced anxiously at each other. The other men were frowning and a short powerful guy stalked to the front door. He crossed thick arms over his chest and scowled at me. In a group, the odd race out always gets the blame.

"We better do something," I said.

"What?" said Luis.

"It must be fast," Javier said. "What makes a man run from his bed?"

"A nightmare."

"A rat bite."

"A fire."

Luis trotted to the kitchen for supplies while his brother soothed the men. The twins brewed a fire in a metal garbage can and blew the smoke through the door into Marduk's room. A styrofoam egg carton released a particularly vile smell. We heard the thump of feet hitting the floor.

Still asleep, Marduk left his room bearing an enormous urinary erection. His knee hit the garbage can and cinders scattered across the floor. The Monster steered Marduk to the bathroom like an oak bowsprit and everyone sighed, listening to the heavy blast of urine. He returned with the Monster sagged to half-mast. Marduk stepped on a hot coal and leaped howling into the smoky air. Long black hair slapped his face. His lingam waved like a palm tree in a typhoon, smacking his belly and thighs, sending everyone in a scramble of flight. As the pain faded, Marduk ceased his wild dance, and staggered into bed.

For the next half hour there was much discussion of what each man would sacrifice to acquire the Monster. Conversation built to a contest until a guy built like an outhouse said he'd give up his life to be buried with such equipment. This silenced the others since nothing could quite top death.

The Minnesota winter lingered deep into spring, encasing the sky with a sunless gray. Men stiffened at Marduk's approach as if he were a decorated colonel among fresh troops. Women were brazen with their eyelashes, or quickly turned away. Marduk saw nothing. He worked part-time at the car wash and in the afternoons made tape recordings of his mother's lessons in traditional life. The weather began to warm. Melted snow ran black along the gutters.

Luis and Javier had been promoted to money runners for a bookie, and now owned one pistol between them. It was an H&R .22 that held eight rounds. The serial number had been filed off so long ago it had blued over. They took turns carrying the gun but refused to include me in the rotation, saying that as lookout I needed to stay clean.

The bookie was a large man who ran a numbers racket, and took bets on horse races in Omaha and Chicago. Everyone called him Mister Turf. He operated from a back room in a bar. All morning four phones rang continually. I'd never seen a toupé before and his was so obvious that I inadvertently laughed the first time I saw it. Mister Turf became quite irate until learning where I was from. He assumed that he had an expert on hand, and thereafter referred to me as his Kentuckian, a term that impressed the twins.

Mister Turf was angry with the city of Minneapolis, which had betrayed him by opening construction on a racetrack in a nearby suburb. Legal gambling would ruin him. Before that occurred, he was intent on saving a stake large enough to start a female mud-wrestling club.

I trailed after Luis and Javier like a pesky younger brother, doing whatever they asked, which was mainly waiting by a pay phone to prevent anyone from using it. After two rings, I picked it up, said "Red dog" into the receiver, and hung up. If the phone rang again, I answered it and wrote down the muttered message—a string of coded numbers. One of the brothers picked up the note and carried it to Mister Turf. Since paper and pencil were required, I had freedom to write in my journal, a practice that slowly began to supersede every aspect of my life. As long as I was able to record events, my shoddy circumstances didn't matter. I began making outlandish statements to passersby simply to provoke a response worthy of logging.

The brothers and I drank every night, and enjoyed free meals in a variety of bars. I ate tongue, dog, horse, and millions of black beans. We planned another *fiesta del monstruo*, but our pleasant life was interrupted by the sudden arrival of Luis and Javier's cousin María.

She was eighteen, lacked legal papers, and was staying with their aunt across town. Aunt Tiamat had been a successful prostitute in the Ecuadorian capital of Quito but was shrewd enough to retire early. Since emigrating to America, she'd helped family members follow. The twins owed her their current bandit status. They, along with others she'd brought to America, gave her a percentage of their income.

The brothers were determined that I should marry María. My shocked refusal meant nothing. They assured me that she was a virgin. At night they plied me with a higher grade of liquor. Hadn't they taken me in like a brother? Wasn't I at this moment drinking their rum?

I explained my devotion to Jennipher in Kentucky. They didn't believe me and made veiled suggestions about my secret racism. I hauled out the wrinkled photo of Jennipher as proof. It was from the sixth grade, when we passed notes reading, "Do You Like Me? Check Yes or No." Her apparent youth upped my waning masculine status. They were stymied until Luis grinned and smacked his brother out of his chair. He spoke rapidly in Spanish, then switched to English.

"That is not here, Kentucky! You can be married in this country and that is one thing. You can have a wife in another country and that is another thing!"

"No, Luis," I said. "Kentucky is in the U.S."

"Now you are lying, Chrissie. You have told us the stories of your country. It is warm and in the mountains. It is far away. The people go in the dirt and make coal."

"We understand that you are nervous," Javier said. "A man is always nervous before his wedding."

"Tomorrow Chrissie will meet María," Luis said to his brother, helping him stand. "Tonight we drink!"

The next morning I awoke hung over and filled with dread. The boys briefed me on Ecuadorian etiquette, which I was determined to violate, thereby dodging matrimony by sheer rudeness. Near dusk we walked the several blocks to Aunt Tiamat's house. Luis and Javier were edgy, intimidated by the prospect of visiting their infamous aunt. I felt calm, knowing that my sojourn in Minneapolis was nearly over.

Aunt Tiamat was tall and elegant and moved with a predatory grace. She was heavy but well proportioned, carrying her weight with the nobility of a veteran wearing medals. She dressed with bold sensuality while obeying the confines of decorum. Cleavage was a reminder, not an invitation. Everyone chatted in Spanish and I nodded like an imbecile. Aunt Tiamat bowed to me and left the room.

"Now you will meet María," Luis whispered.

"She is our cousin."

"Aunt Tiamat is our aunt."

"You are stupid!" Javier said. "Chrissie is not stupid. He knows who is who."

Outside, a freight train moved through town, its whistle a sound of mourning. I was trapped without a Cumberland Gap in sight, stuck like Boone with a local squaw.

Aunt Tiamat glided regally into the room and presented María like a valuable flintlock in red high heels. She was petite and brown with a breast-tilt that defied gravity. Each ankle was thin as a worry line. María was at her maiden's peak and I knew how Daniel had felt when he saw the purity of untouched land.

Luis and Javier stood stiff-backed as southern gentlemen until Aunt Tiamat dismissed them with a slight gesture of her wrist. They sidled out the door, winking at me. She led María away and returned to pour two brandies. After a sip, she spoke.

"María says she is in love with you."

"What!"

"Because you will marry her."

"I won't."

"You must."

"Why?"

"Because she is in love with you."

For a few minutes I pondered the idea, thinking of those red high heels. I could pass her off as Shawnee in Kentucky and we'd live on rice and beans. My family would understand. We're flexible in the hills. One of Rebecca Boone's babies was fathered by Daniel's brother, the penalty for her husband's wandering.

Aunt Tiamat refilled our glasses. Regardless of María's beauty, I didn't want a wife of convenience. As businessmen, Luis and Javier could understand my refusal, but they'd consider it a betrayal of their aunt's decree, a stake higher than their own honor. It was time to use the lessons they'd taught me.

"Marduk is better," I said. "He's learning Spanish."

"Who?"

"The Indian. You know."

I spread my hands to indicate size. Her eyes narrowed and the glass trembled slightly in her hand.

"*El monstruo*," she said.

"Yup."

"It is true?"

"Yup."

"He would be too much for María."

"But not for you. He could marry María and live here. She'll get citizenship." I stepped close, dizzied by her perfume, and slowly flipped my hole card.

"Marduk has never been with a woman."

Aunt Tiamat gripped a chairback, her eyes wide as castanets. A faint seam of perspiration gleamed along her upper lip.

"Take me to him," she said. "You must keep my nephews away this night."

She telephoned for a taxi and didn't speak during the ride. I let her in our hovel. She handed me a wad of bills and shooed me away. In a nearby bar Luis and Javier were drinking with a pair of neighborhood hookers. The brothers met me at the door.

"It's settled," I said. "Aunt Tiamat gave me money to celebrate. How much do they want?"

We looked across the dim room at the whores.

"Twenty," said Luis.

"And mine is worth thirty."

"Then I believe," Luis said, "that mine is worth forty."

"Mine wants forty-five."

"You two stay here," I said.

For a hundred bucks and a bottle of rum, the women promised to keep them until noon the next day. Luis hugged me. Javier hugged me, then kissed me on the cheek. Luis pushed his brother aside, lifted me off the floor, and kissed me on both cheeks. Javier reached for me. I ran for the door, wiping beer spittle off my face.

Boone probably kissed a favorite hound dog but never another man.

In the street I realized that I had nowhere to go for the night, and would have to leave town. I snuck into our apartment for my belongings. Marduk's bed thumped in time to his wailing Chippewa song, Geb finally opening the matrix of Nut. I filled my backpack and walked across town beneath a full moon flat as a tortilla in the cloudless sky. María opened the door.

"*Mi novia*," she murmured.

I embraced her and we mangled each other on the couch. Either María had lied to the twins or they had lied to me; she was no virgin. We fit together like Lincoln logs. When the calamity was over and María lay nestled against me, I began thinking of water and movement. Tomorrow Minnesota and its thousand lakes would be one more place to which I'd never return.

Daniel Boone came home once a year to rest, resulting in sixteen kids. The same year that Kentucky honored him by giving a county his name, two sheriffs stole ten thousand acres of his land to sell for taxes. He left the state in 1799, feeling crowded by the appearance of a new neighbor twenty miles away. At age eighty-five, he died the hero's death—choking to death on a sweet potato.

Rising at sunup, I dressed and fixed a cup of coffee. María found me in the kitchen lacing my boots. Sunlight polished her mahogany skin and winked on the curls below her flat belly. Chilly air starched her nipples. She stepped forward, slapped me across the face, kissed me quickly, and ran from the room. The ghost of Daniel whispered that I should leave. Not being Quaker like Boone, Luis and Javier's method of vengeance might include all eight bullets from the little .22. I stepped into the dawn streets and walked to the meat market, where a trucker carried me west.

Summer for me has always been a time of hibernation, a hallucinatory season to be endured. This one is passing in a fury of photosynthesis and intimacy. Rita has kept her job for the insurance, while her belly grows. A small magazine has accepted a short story and sent me a check for fifty-four dollars. It's my third publication, the first that paid. Rita is happy. The check validates her decision to have a child with me, proves that my days as a bum are gone. I take her to town for dinner. The bill is low since Rita is eating five small meals a day instead of three large ones.

The rest of the money buys fabric to make curtains for the baby's room. After borrowing a sewing machine, I manage to produce two hemmed strips that will fit no window in the house. They hang at a slant. Sunlight borders the sides; the bottom is eight inches below the windowsill. I am prouder of them than of getting published.

Every morning I take coffee to the river and sit in the same chair where I ended the previous night with beer. I prop my feet on a sandbag left from the flood. Now, in late July, drought is killing the corn, and the river has dwindled to a creek. The morning stillness is broken only by the symphony of birds claiming turf, and my neighbor's boat as he checks his catfish lines. To him the river is a tool. He's trapped and fished it for two decades.

Twenty-five hundred years ago, a Greek named Heraclitus said, "You can't step into the same river twice." I climb down the bank and remove my shoes and socks. The river is warm on my skin, a continuous flow that is immediately gone, yet remains. The water surrounding one leg is not the same as around the other leg. Sediment drifts away and it occurs to me that you can't even step on the same bank twice. Each footstep alters the earth.

Heraclitus is known as "the Obscure" because none of his writings survived. My neighbor has no use for his ideas. To him the river is always the same, moving past his house, providing food. He steps into it every day. He gauges the spots to set his poles by the texture of mud beneath his feet. I spread my legs as far as I can. One foot is Heraclitus, the other is my neighbor. I am floating somewhere in between. Wind in the high boughs makes the leaves ripple like water, producing a distant whisper. Fish eggs cling to rock along the shore.

Rita's eggs are thirty-four years old. She wanted amnioscentesis to eliminate the worry of producing a baby less than perfect. Her uncles, aunts, cousins, and grandparents all died in World War II—some in combat, some in death camps. Rita can never be sure what genetic oddities run in the family. Her feet are flat and she has dyslexia. One of my eyes is farsighted, the other nearsighted. As a kid, I had big teeth bucked so badly that four molars were yanked to make room.

Standing in the river, I imagine DNA as something large and visible, extending from throat to navel, full of unruly tangles that produce cowlicks, walleyes, and pinheads. I was against the test, afraid that if our child turned out damaged, it would mean that I was too. Even worse, if the results showed a Down's baby, I would want to keep it anyway. The test is for throwing it back.

Rita prevailed and two weeks ago, we went to the hospital. She was told to drink sixteen ounces of juice. Half an hour later a nurse strapped her to a table. Above Rita's head sat a sonogram screen that would monitor the probing of her gut. The nurse lifted Rita's shirt, pulled her pants down, and swabbed her belly with a clear gel. She nodded to the doctor, another woman, who pressed an ultrasound transducer to Rita's stomach. The sonogram screen filled with a murky, mobile image that looked nothing like a child. The white areas were tissue, the black was fluid. The spine looked like a zipper. The doctor measured the skull and thigh. She checked the heart, which was working fine. Flowing along the top of the image were horizontal layers of uterine wall and placenta, bringing to mind a summer sunset, changing with the light of the heart.

The doctor manipulated the sonogram until two vertical images bisected the screen. She froze one, enlarged the other, and took photographs. "There's a hand," she said, indicating a pale blot. "We're looking at the baby as if it was sitting in a chair and we're underneath. It's mooning us. The legs are crossed, so we can't see the genitals. It's shy."

I watched the screen, trying to see as the doctor did, but found only a shifting landscape of black and white, a bubbling tar pit that caught light and held bones. "It looks good," she said. "Fifteen-point-nine weeks along."

She pressed several buttons and changed the image to a cone that represented a three-dimensional cross section inside Rita's belly. As the doctor moved the transducer, the image in the cone changed. She was hunting for a large space, far from the fetus, close to the amniotic wall. "There's one," she said. "Perfect."

The screen showed a dark gap surrounded by gray and white like an astronomical photograph. The nurse handed her a syringe. The needle was very long, a beak. She used both hands to insert it into a guiding tube that was pressed tight to Rita's belly. Rita closed her eyes. The doctor watched the monitor, moving her hands by rote, pushing the needle into darkness.

"Tenting," she said, and the nurse repeated the word. I asked what it meant.

The nurse explained that the amnion was tough enough to resist the needle; it was like pressing a stick against the wall of a tent. After several tries, the doctor breached the amnion. The syringe sucked pale liquid into its chamber, and I had a sudden impulse to drink it. My knees felt trembly. A gray fog crowded my vision. The nurse took my arm and led me to a chair, advising me to place my head between my legs. She cleaned Rita's stomach. The final image on the monitor showed a section of Rita's interior in the shape of a cornucopia, the horn of life.

We drove home and Rita went to bed. For two hours I watched

her sleep. The baby was missing an ounce of life already, a shot glass of amniotic fluid, and I was afraid that it might notice. We had taken its water away, like drought. I sat on the bed and apologized to Rita's belly for our invasion.

The two-week wait went slowly. Today's mail should contain the results of our amnio. I leave the river and climb the bank to my chair. Maples crowd the opposite bank, their leaves tinted yellow by lack of rain. The yard is brown and I think of lush summers in the hills at home. The grass is always greener where people die young. Our child is an underground spring straining at the confluence of Rita and me. The amnio will tell us if it's polluted.

The river is sinking like a lost continent, a misplacement for which we all suffer. Yesterday I took the boat out, but a light breeze halted me in a holding pattern between current and wind. I had to wade home, pulling the boat with a rope, wondering how much further the river can shallow itself. Maps show it as a thin blue line the color of a vein until oxygen turns it the hue of mud. Should drought drink all the water, the other side of the river would still be this side. Herons would lose their safety, and bridges would have no meaning. If the waterways lay empty to the sea, the ocean would run backwards into the vacant riverbeds, rubbing salt against the open wounds of earth. Drought and flood, that slow sabotage of the soul, would never matter again. The dam that holds nothing back becomes a tombstone for the river.

At two in the afternoon I fill a canteen with water and walk the half mile to my mailbox on the blacktop. The dirt road bisects a cornfield that is, as the farmers say, "standing dead." Each step raises a plume of dust beneath my foot. I stop three times to sip water in the oppressive heat of prairie summer. The handle of the mailbox burns my hand. Inside are two bills, a newspaper from Kentucky, and a rejected story. The amnio results are in a plain brown envelope, which I carry carefully, holding it away from my body like a snake. The mail is damp from sweat by the time I reach the house.

When Rita comes home from work, she makes me open the envelope. There is a four-by-four-inch photograph of the baby's chromosomes separated into pairs like matching flatworms. An accompanying letter says that the test has shown them to be structurally sound. The kid has a solid foundation. If it turns out to be a terrorist, the fault will be environmental, not genetic. Rita and I hug each other for what seems like hours. Her eyes are damp. I sense that I want to cry, but something deep inside forbids it, like a safety on a rifle, or a childproof cap. I cannot muster the courage of release.

I go to the room we've prepared for the baby. In the center stands a white bassinet, a lidless picnic basket on legs, the same one I slept in as a newborn. My mother insisted on shipping it from the mountains to the prairie. She'd kept it, she said, against this very time. The bassinet is curved into an oval the shape of an egg. The light is dim. Everything has been placed with care. The whole room has an ethereal, expectant quality, like that of a cathedral in which miracles are rumored to occur.

I was my parents' first child and it occurs to me that my father must have regarded this same bassinet with similar trepidation. I suddenly realize that I've been misreading the myth of Oedipus all my life. Drinking mother's milk does not beget a thirst for father's blood. The tragedy belongs to Laius, the father. Oedipus didn't fulfill his own destiny, he lived up to his father's terror.

I step outside to sit by the river in the streaming red light of summer dusk. Mosquitoes are working hard. I've hung old gourds on a frame to attract swifts because they feed on mosquitoes, but the birds care little for such accommodation. A great horned owl delivers a bellow that hushes the floodplain woods. A light rain blows downriver, a few sprinkles that pass rapidly as blown confetti.

The pregnancy is four months along, five to go. Rita dozes on the couch. The embryo has already set cells aside for its own offspring, like a farmer saving seed corn for next year's crop. Female mosquitoes land on my skin, needing fresh blood for their young.

The guts of America unfolded in every direction as I traveled the interstate bloodstream, dodging the white corpuscles of perverts, cops, and outlaws. Thumbing induced a peculiar form of freedom linked to terror. I could go anywhere, sleep anywhere, be killed anywhere. The only restrictions were fear and rain. Mine was the indifferent life of a barnacle: temporary attachment to a larger object at a pace dependent upon the ride. Lacking plan or destination, I was at last content. A job became as meaningless as food and shelter, a drab necessity.

I was roaming with my brethren, all the ragtag bums and bandits moving through the nation. Occasionally we met at a cloverleaf. After a visual sizing up, in which each of us tried to look menacing in case the other was an escaped convict, we claimed our hitching spots. Existence was reduced to a backpack, the highway, and the benevolence of utter strangers. I kept my journal buttoned inside my shirt. The pack and everything in it could be abandoned.

I slalomed the past, searching for a genetic base to my wandering. Dad had grown up in a genuine log cabin and had inherited a fraction of crackpottery. My own fisticuffs with the world proved that I bore my generation's share of the family darkness. When I was twelve, Dad quit his job as a traveling salesman and came home for good. He grew a beard and wore mail order African dashikis. He tuned in to distant airwaves, turned on with bourbon, and dropped into the family. Our absent father had become a stranger who never left the house.

My brother and I spent all our time outside playing baseball, using plates from the kitchen as bases. Soon we ran out of plates, a fact that Mom accepted with an equanimity fed by years of facing cryptic boy-stuff. Lacking brothers, she'd had no experience with young boys. She was like a straw boss of immigrant workers—she didn't speak our language, and regarded our alien ways as best left alone. Mom preferred not to tell Dad about the plate shortage until he was in a receptive mood, a wait that could conceivably require the passage of a season. He'd blame her, and we were too broke to buy new dishes.

Mom's grand solution was paper plates. She'd gotten hold of a dozen somehow, probably through VISTA, since they prowled the hills giving away combs, key chains, and toothbrushes. To make the paper plates last, we used them over and over until they were heavy as hubcaps. Every Saturday we ate fried chicken, Dad's favorite meal. For dessert he split the bones and sucked the marrow. He finally lifted his plate for seconds and the bottom dropped like a trapdoor, dumping his cache of bones to the table. He immediately accused me of having booby-trapped his plate.

"No," I said. "Mine's the same way."

I lifted my plate and a chunk of mashed potato slid through the opening. My siblings followed suit, attempting to head off Dad's phenomenal and unpredictable rage. When he got mad, which was not infrequent, the house was tense as a cancer ward until everyone apologized. To avoid these awful times, we coalesced to maintain the illusion of normalcy at any cost.

Dad hunched his bony shoulders, preparing for either a ten-hour tirade or face-saving laughter. His greatest fear was of duplicating Caesar's deathbed epiphany, and each of us was a potential Brutus, Judas, or Delilah. Everyone looked at Mom. Affairs didn't often come to this, but when they did, her reaction was crucial. She hated to take a side. Her usual stance was a balancing act between loyalty to her children and to her husband. She raised us, but Dad controlled us. If so much as a hound dog refused fealty, it disappeared in a South American fashion and was never mentioned.

Mom calmly tipped over a bowl of peaches. Thick juice ran across the old formica. Dad plucked a peach from the table and ate it. I stuffed a handful of beans down my gullet and we finished the meal eating like Romans.

It was late that night, lying in bed, when I decided to save my money and head into the world.

A decade later I was in it, facing the end of autumn. During cold weather bums and birds headed south, and I wintered in West Texas, working as a painter of houses built rapidly during the oil boom. Entire towns were materializing near oilfields. Trucks brought stud walls and rafter frames, predrilled for electrical wires. Young trees waited for holes, their root balls wrapped in cheesecloth. Mats of damp sod arrived by flatbed truck. As soon as the interior work was complete, a family moved into the house.

Outdoor painting was the last stage, and I hired with a contractor named Bill, a former gunnery sergeant in Vietnam. Half the crew was Mexican and the rest were ex-cons or marginal ruffians. Bill paid us in cash at the end of each day, saying, "You have two choices, boys. You can save for a convertible or spend it on poontang. I'll go your bail once. Just once."

Bill always wore some article of military clothing—a hat one day, boots the next, a web belt on another day. He was prone to silent crying, apropos of nothing. No one mentioned it. He was also good-looking and gentle, very popular with the women whose houses we colored. After an incident in which a woman exposed her breasts to me while I was on a ladder, I asked him if he'd ever gotten laid on a job.

"The problem is what to do with your wet brush," he said. "If you lay it on top of the bucket, it gets too dry. And if you stick it in the bucket, the paint gets up into the handle and ruins the bristles." He glanced at the bleak landscape beyond the carefully watered lawns. "Indoor work with latex is the best."

The woman whose house we were painting couldn't decide what color she wanted. We had several different buckets, and were instructed to paint giant swatches on the front of the house. After lunch, the crew lounged in the shade while the other wives in the community congregated to give opinion. They carried infants, whom they regarded with the same detachment as they did the patches of color on the siding.

"You know, Judy's baby has already got a suntan," one mother said. "I'm going to get mine in the sun today."

"I can't make mine shut up crying long enough to dress it," said another.

"Take and push half a Tylenol up its butt. That quiets mine right down. Regular, not extra-strength."

The husbands took little interest in their homes, confining their aesthetic concerns to clothing. Boot toes ran to amazing points, as if designed to spindle a spider in a corner. They wore the biggest hats in the West, decorated with huge feathers. In local bars, the men spent most of their time accusing each other of having "knocked my feather." Such an insult was tantamount to a Kentucky warning shot, the French musketeer's slap in the face, or the New York faux pas of daring to look someone in the eyes for more than ten seconds.

"Hey!" someone would yell. "You knocked my feather."

People backed away from the victim, who stroked his feather while glaring at the perpetrator. The accused man stared back. Each stretched his body to full height, squinting, jaw thrust out, gauging his chances in case things got downright western. After a minute of staring, both men turned slowly away feigning reluctance. After witnessing this rite, I spoke with the men involved. Each claimed to be a descendant of original settlers. One was a dentist. The other worked as an accountant. Both were a little put out that oil hadn't been discovered on their land.

When occasional trouble actually erupted, it was the wrestling-across-the-floor sort, until one man exposed his genitals in surrender. A little while later they'd be drinking together. The Kentucky style of brawling is similar to the Viking berserker—all out, using whatever is at hand, aiming for the throat and crotch. Texans seemed to consider anything shy of a gunfight little more than sport.

Since I couldn't trust myself to follow house rules, I spent the better part of four months dodging feathers.

After work one Friday, Bill and I were in a tavern drinking beer and shooting pool. A neckless man with a body like a wedge called Bill a feather knocker. Bill turned away. The man followed, saying that Bill was a chicken with a yellow stripe up his back a mile wide. There were three guys backing him up. As casually as possible, I picked up an empty beer mug in each hand. Bill saw me and shook his head. The man stepped close, yelling so fiercely that saliva sprayed the air. Bill leaned to the man, their chests nearly touching, and began talking in a low voice. Then he walked back to the pool table and sank a combination shot as if he'd been concentrating on the game all along. The other man stood immobile for a couple of minutes before returning to his bar stool.

I asked Bill what he'd said.

"Simple," he said. "I told him that if we fought, all we'd do was rip our clothes, and women didn't favor men wearing tore-up shirts. I said there was nothing wrong with fighting but I didn't feel like it today."

"That's all it took?"

"No," Bill said. "I kindly had hold of his balls the whole time, squeezing tighter and tighter."

After the war, Bill had stayed drunk for three years, then tried the rodeo circuit as a bull rider. He described it as wrapping your arm around a chain tied to the bumper of a car, then having the driver pop the clutch. The first two seconds were the worst. It didn't compare to the exhilaration of combat, though, and it wasn't until recently that he'd found an activity that did.

Twice a month, Bill went skydiving. He offered to pay the fee if I accompanied him, and we drove an hour to a small airstrip near a cattle ranch. Two other customers were there. Like us, one was an aficionado, the other a novice. An instructor outfitted us with boots and coveralls, then spent two hours teaching us to land and roll.

The four of us flew into the sky with the instructor. The main chute was strapped to my back. A spare on my chest made me realize the extent to which I'd finally taken the irrational. The little plane leveled out at three thousand feet, circling above a scrubby pasture. The noise made talking impossible. Wind rushed through the open hatch. Bill winked at me and left the aircraft half a mile above the earth. He was simply not there anymore. I knew instantly that this was the stupidest idea I'd ever had. I decided to stay in the plane, and shifted position to go last so the others would not witness my decision. Once they were gone, I'd feign cramps, a headache, or a case of the vapors.

The second man gave his buddy the thumbs-up signal and jumped. The next guy balked at the door. He fought the instructor, kicking and scrabbling, and huddled in the rear of the fuselage, his face wet with tears. The instructor looked at me, shrugged, and rolled his eyes. I realized that I had to go. I wasn't as afraid as the other guy, but the instructor's look of contempt would place me in the same category. Very slowly, I moved to the hatch.

Ten million years of genetic conditioning screamed in outrage and protest. Every molecule in me forbade the jump. I gripped a handle beside the door and closed my eyes. The plane was shaking and so were my knees, but I was too scared to be a coward. I leaned through the hole. Open fields flashed below. Free-fall lasted all of four seconds, but they were long ones, rushing to earth at thirty-two feet per second. I yelled and the rush of air kept my mouth wide. The chute jerked open with a hard thump, and I squeezed the ropes as tightly as possible. There was a brief period of intense joy in which I realized that the only way to increase the feeling was to jump from higher up. Briefly I wished we had. I was already halfway down, and instead of wafting like a leaf, I seemed to be dropping at an incredible rate. Some huge mechanism was pushing the land rapidly in my direction.

I hit the earth, rolled as I'd been taught, and came up covered with flakes of last year's cow droppings. Wind caught the parachute and wrapped me with lines. Bill bounded across the field, his face stained with manure.

"Did you piss?" he yelled.

I was so grateful to be sitting in dirt that I didn't understand what he was talking about. He helped me out of the straps. I could smell dust and urine.

"I knew you would," he said, pointing to the wet fly of my coveralls. "Some guys load their britches. It happens at impact. After another couple of jumps, you won't anymore."

A waiting truck trundled us back to the airstrip. When the plane landed, the guy who'd stayed aboard climbed out with his head down. No one looked at him. His presence was a reminder of our own unclaimed fear.

Bill clapped me across the shoulders. "That's why you have to pay in advance," he said. "Next time you and me'll go at a higher altitude."

He told me about his first brush with the enemy, an experience that had led him to reenlist. He was the first man behind the soldier walking point, leading their platoon through jungle. The point man gave the hand signal for VC and motioned Bill forward. Six enemy were walking toward a pond in a clearing at the bottom of the slight hill. They each carried a bucket in one hand, a weapon in the other.

The point man whispered to Bill, "Cover me with single fire. I'll be on rock and roll."

When the hostiles moved close, the point man began spraying bursts of automatic fire. Bill plugged away. His last thought, he told me, was wishing he was the one who got to use automatic. It seemed like more fun. After that, he always volunteered to walk point.

A month later, Bill didn't show up for work, an unprecedented event. He didn't answer the phone and none of us knew where he lived. A police car arrived at the work site. The cop told us that the night before, Bill had removed his clothes and stacked them neatly. He then drank a pint of kerosene, and Zippoed his mouth—reversing the favored method of Vietnamese monks protesting the war. There was no note.

He'd once told me that when a man died in combat, the survivors never eulogized him. Instead they insulted him for days, talking about how well rid they were of his presence, no matter how close they'd been. I considered taking his paintbrush, but decided it would be an affront. Sentiment, he'd said, only made you vulnerable.

I aimed myself north, a tricky move without benefit of interstates. Five days later a gay black man picked me up at an isolated exit along the North Platte River in Nebraska. He claimed to eat white boys like me for lunch. I told him I wasn't fit for a meal. He laughed and left my lingam alone, nestled and trembling deep in its fur. A cornholing on the road was my greatest fear, worse than murder. He said his single regret was being born black in the South instead of red on the Plains, because the Indians accepted homosexuality in a more civilized manner. Then he laughed and said it really didn't matter because they both got fucked hard.

He dropped me off near Omaha, where I found slaughterhouse work, herding huge steers down a narrow ramp to death. They walked steadily, without curiosity or comprehension. A man placed an electrical rod against their foreheads and literally zapped the crap out of them. It was boring and professional; at home we used a rifle. After one stench-filled day, I quit and walked to the vacant prairie at the edge of town, hoping to hear a coyote. There was nothing but bugs. Constellations spanned the sky. The moon moldered like a gnawed bone. Two hundred years back, someone asked Boone if he had ever been lost. He answered no, but that he'd once been bewildered for three days. I knew exactly how he felt.

Buried beneath my sleeping bag lay dinosaur bones mixed with bison, antelope, and Sioux. The barometer of intelligence is the innate ability to adapt, to tame for the conqueror. Maybe wild and dead was better, like bison, Crazy Horse, and wolves. I watched the sky, wondering if I was living at the edge of adaptability, cherishing the residue of death.

I thought of Bill's belief that America's greatest contributions to world culture came from the West.

"The all-night diner," he'd said. "And the billboard. You can get coffee and talk at any time you want. The billboard always tells you where you are."

"Time and space. Cowboy science."

"That's what I like about you, Chris. You're so damn dumb you don't know you're smart. Like Mr. Charles in the Nam."

He turned his head slightly away, enough so that I knew to avert my gaze. The tears were coming down his face. His breathing was normal and he didn't sob. It was as if his head was so filled with sorrow that it had sprung a couple of leaks. When it passed he looked at me, his eyes hard and ancient as a trilobite's. "The West wasn't tamed," he said. "It was corralled for slaughter."

I woke early and on the move, despising Nebraskans for their cultural politesse. A man couldn't buy a pack of smokes without being offered a lighter, exhorted to have a good day, and in general made to feel inferior for not being aggressively cheerful enough. Nebraska was symmetric as an equation, the pathetic result of living on land emptied of buffalo. Prairie dog towns had been reduced to tourist attractions.

I tarried hard in the West, eager to find a home. American boys are raised knowing that a horse between your legs and a low-slung pistol are a guarantee of manhood. It worked for Billy the Kid, who shot seventeen men in the back before he reached legal age. Montana was a beautiful state, but lacked employment. I met a guy with a graduate degree who felt lucky to have work mending fence. A waitress told me that if I planned to settle there, I should bring a woman with me. I was unable to find work in Wyoming either, which made me want to stay, believing that the citizens shared my propensity for freedom. The difference was that they had places to sleep. The people were open to strangers, perhaps because they saw so few. Instead of viewing me with eastern scorn or southern suspicion, they recognized me for what I was, more or less a damn fool.

In Colorado I got a job chipping mortar from bricks with a hammer and chisel. I sat in the dirt beside a pile of brick, making a new pile in a primitive form of recycling. The wage was fourteen cents a brick. After two days of squatting in the sun, my hands ached from gripping the tools, and my fingers were scabbed from mislicks with the hammer.

I collected my pay and moved south, crisscrossing the Continental Divide, trying to find the actual border. Rivers run east on one side, west on the other. My goal was to straddle it. Since we are three-quarters water, I figured that the simultaneous tow of both oceans would rip a hole in my soul for something worthwhile to enter. Black Elk said the central mountain is everywhere. From my vantage alone in the Rockies, centrality always seemed elsewhere. More and more, I depended on my journal. It was organic, I believed, even sentient. I came to regard the process of recording a lived life as the only material fit for writing. Somewhere in the Rockies, this shifted into a belief that the journal was my life, and the rest of existence only a fiction.

After two days of walking south, I was lucky enough to catch a ride to Flagstaff, and from there found a job washing dishes at the Grand Canyon. The administrative staff took my photograph and sent me to a lightless cabin with no water. Each morning I joined the other workers in public showers at the end of our dead-end lane. At night we drank in the employee bar.

Washing dishes was the ideal work of freedom, requiring no focus save the immediate cleaning of a mottled pot or plate. It also provided food. The occupation was of such wretched status that no one bothered me. Cooks labored in hundred-degree temperatures, while busboys staggered beneath enormous loads. The best waiters were able to change demeanor extremely fast. Seconds after battling a cook or debasing themselves before a tyrannical boss, they had to be sweetly sensitive to a customer. Bartenders enjoyed a slightly higher rank, but the job entailed steady recruitment and coddling of one's private circle of alcoholics. The dishwasher, in his perpetually soggy and food-flecked state, could remain true to himself.

The canyon gift shops employed Hopi women who sold copper-hued plastic dolls dressed in fringed felt. The hollow foot of each bore an inked stamp that read "Made in Japan." A few yards away was a hole in the ground a mile deep and ten miles wide. Somebody jumped once a month. Every week, a foreign tourist clutching a camera raced through the pines with skunk stench trailing behind. Apparently the Old World has not a polecat to its name. They are cute, graceful creatures, ripe for a photograph. Sometimes an entire family received the spray.

After supper I watched the sunset from the canyon's rim, sitting on the narrowest lip of rock protruding over the hole. I wrote in my diary there, looking down on clouds, trying to understand the strange impulse to step into space. It was not death that pulled me, it was the canyon itself. A jump was an urge to fill the void. Just before dusk, I witnessed an electrical storm from above, actually seeing the ignition of lightning and smelling the discharge. A sudden lance of fire cracked into the canyon's bowels and disappeared. The air smelled of ozone. It cured me of the itch to jump.

Weekends, I walked to the bottom where the Colorado River continued to cut a path. The river has never actually sunk but remains in place, cutting the land as the earth rises against the water. My treks down were a passage backwards through time, descending through millennia layered in the geology of the canyon walls. Color marked each era. Red at the top faded to pink, brown, a delicate green, and finally the slates and violets of the bottom. Naturally there was a bar and restaurant beside the river. Every Sunday, I climbed out to my work.

I was the only dishwasher who was not black, Mexican, or Indian. We worked in teams posted at either end of a colossal automatic washer and rinser. One man fed the beast while two others stacked the clean plates. A fourth dried silverware. Since I was new, my chore was the worst—scraping food into plastic barrels. I saved the good parts to divide later among the crew. Willie, the head cook, offered me a job as short-order breakfast cook. I refused, preferring the simple world of water and dishes. Willie didn't quite understand this. Each day, he asked if I'd changed my mind yet. He eventually offered a higher wage, but I remained loyal to freedom.

A new manager was shifted to the restaurant, a sneering spud named Jackie Jr. Like many dwellers of the West, he pretended to be a cowboy, in hand-tooled boots, expensive hats, and tailored shirts with pearl snaps. Accustomed to calling all dishwashers "boy," Jackie Jr. enjoyed referring to me as a "hillbilly," a term that put me off my feed. Hillbilly was what the people in town called us at home; that and worse—hick, ridgerunner, redneck, inbred ingrate, and my personal favorite, pigfucker. My mother is my sixth cousin. My brother and sister are also my cousins but nobody in my family ever seduced a hog.

I decided to quit after a week beneath the rule of Jackie Jr. On my final shift, he sauntered through the kitchen, amused at our miserable condition. I turned off the dishwashing machine and told him it was broken.

"What's the matter, hillfuck?" he said. "Even Meskins know how to crank this sucker on."

As he pushed the mechanized button, I opened the metal trapdoor that housed the soap jets. Jackie Jr. screeched like a kicked cat. Suds and water ruined his splendid clothes. I stepped past him and out the back door, where my pack waited beside a dumpster surrounded by skunks and ravens. Willie followed me. I turned with my arms spread and low, unsure what to expect. His face was lined as a washboard. He eyed the backpack strapped to my shoulders, opened his wallet, and handed me two twenty-dollar bills.

"Go while you can, kid. I'll slow him down some."

"I don't need your money, Willie."

"Don't be a fool, kid. You're too puny to back it up." He shook his head, chuckling. "I was a goddam drifter once."

He waited till I took the money, then stepped into the kitchen. I tried to imagine white-haired Willie being young. It was easier than seeing myself as old. I'd begun traveling with the vague belief that I sought something tangible. Now I wondered if I was actually running away, not toward. The legendary West, with its vast and empty spaces, had boiled down to just that—vast and empty, filled with people trying desperately to plug the gap with labor.

I carried my backpack to the single road that led away from the canyon's south rim. In another era, Bill might have been a Texas Ranger fighting the Comanche, or a mountain man scouting the Rockies. People of the West suffer from a historical malady similar to that of Appalachians. They are deprived of the old outlets, but stuck with the need to live up to their heritage.

While waiting for a ride out of the park, I resolved to live in the West—settle rather than pass through—but not yet. I was still an outrider of the self. If I stayed, I knew that I'd become a feral hermit, climbing like the end of a species to higher ground. I didn't want my bones discovered on a rocky ledge at thin altitude. There was still California to explore, the edge of the continent.

Summer has faded deep into autumn, the days collapsing into darkness at either end. Beneath the changing leaves, I split firewood and gather kindling. Rita's hair is lustrous, her nails strong. My winter beard is growing in. Come spring, I will shed it for another six months. Yesterday I watched a blue jay tamping weeds over a supply of acorns, hopping as if to flatten the earth above a grave. Today a squirrel has found the cache. The river is afloat with geese possessing the obstinacy of bison aiming their bodies into wind. Cattle die doing that.

I have read every pregnancy book in the library, all of which are naturally geared toward women. The most progressive include a short chapter on the man's role at the end of the book. There is invariably a photo of a virile-looking man with a mustache who is changing a diaper. A woman smiles in the background.

The mother bear will fight to the death for her cubs while her mate wanders the mountain. The female eagle is larger than the male, and in her passion can accidentally kill him during copulation. A buck deer thinks nothing of sending his harem forward as a decoy to ensure the safety of his travel. All this sounds good to me, but Rita and I are evolved. She is not a gatherer. I no longer hunt. The fact is, I'm home all the time, deep in my private cave, blowing red ochre onto blank pages.

Expectant fathers are encouraged to clean the house, cook meals, and tell their wives how lovely they look while carrying forty extra pounds. One book admonishes me not to rush Rita into sex after delivery. Another suggests that I refuse to sleep through the night until the baby does, a period that might last a year. This is to help me bond with my kid, implying that an infant born prior to this book was insufficiently connected to its daddy. Fathers are at fault in everything; even God let his son die.

Women of my mother's generation were drugged during labor. When Mom awakened, the doctor gave her the swaddled gift of me. Dad was kept isolated until a nurse came for him with that immortal phrase, "It's a boy." His first view of me was through a pane of glass. Dad has since told me that I was bright red and screaming, and that he asked the nurse if maybe the quiet one wasn't his instead. Mom has said that she didn't remember much for a couple of days.

For Rita and me, choosing to have children in our mid-thirties requires Lamaze, a role reversal for each of us. I am to be sensitive and encouraging while Rita's goal is a terse machismo. Our Lamaze class meets in a hospital waiting room, which has so few chairs that pregnant women are forced to sit on the floor. Orderlies tramp in to buy drinks from a machine. The instructor's attitude suggests that we are part of a select birth cult and should be proud of inclusion. Again and again she emphasizes the pain of birth, saying it is similar to having your lips peeled over your head. She cannot demonstrate relaxation techniques because she's wearing a dress.

"In the old days in Iowa," she tells us, "women rode off on horseback to have the baby alone. A few hours later they came home with the new baby. I can't imagine that ride back, can you?" She releases a smug giggle. "You'll understand after you give birth."

She separates the couples and asks the men to make a list of negative qualities about their wives during pregnancy. We are leery and resentful of such a chore. Most of us are worried about money, and no one is willing to denounce his wife. Ten minutes later the instructor asks for a volunteer to read our inventory.

"Our wives," begins our spokesman, "are grumpy, sleepy, dopey, happy, bashful, and sneezy." He gestures to the husband of a neurologist. "His wife's doc."

"Very good," the instructor says. "After all the babies are born, we'll get together for a reunion."

The instructor turns the lights off, plays a tape of whales' mating calls, and urges us to meditate.

On the drive home, Rita starts to cry. She feels terrorized by the instructor rather than soothed. She doesn't like having her body referred to as a building with ground floor, basement, boiler room, subcellar, and crawl space. Rita thinks Lamaze is a con job designed to prove how tough females should be. Women are encouraged to undergo tremendous pain, as if to earn their womanhood and deserve a baby. Lamaze focuses outwards, divorcing Rita from the event. She prefers to stay abreast of delivery. I go along with everything.

The next day Rita calls the hospital to change classes, but they're filled and we can't get a refund. Family life has taken its first economic toll. We borrow books and a videotape from the library. I make flashcards depicting the stages of labor and their attendant warning signs. The next morning I leave Rita to the video and go to the woods.

I am unable to walk quietly along the crackling floor of fallen leaves. Birds and animals drift away. Flattened leaves mark a common trail, while kicked leaves turned damp-side up indicate fresh tracks. A heron is poised upriver, leaning like an Eskimo fisherman waiting hours with a spear, as if the wait itself is more important than the hunt. A helicopter seeking crops of marijuana churns the sky. The startled heron lofts awkwardly from shore, stick legs dangling like twin contrails. Trees along the river are so splashed with autumn color that I imagine the pilot has dumped paint from the chopper.

In ancient Mesopotamia agricultural societies worshiped the goddess. Female priests used the serpent as their symbol. Its habit of shedding a skin was physical evidence of birth and rebirth, the moon's ebb and growth, the sow and reap of crop. Fierce nomads eventually arrived from the desert, hunting tribes ruled by men with male deities. They took the land and created the myth of the Fall to punish women for their power. We have been killing snakes ever since. Mother Earth became Papa Sun. Jesus performed the dream of many men—he broke a hymen from the inside out and took up with a hooker. Women want a friend as mate. Men want a virgin in public and a whore in the bedroom, both named Mary of course.

My mother raised the children and took care of the house, as Rita's mother did. Our fathers held employment, carried out the trash, mowed the yard. Life was very simple. Both of our mothers were unhappy.

I am dead set against day care, but know I'll lose, because Rita won't give up her career. She's been at it fifteen years, caring for the mentally ill. She doesn't want to be like her mother, and I don't want to be my father. This opens the possibility of caring for the baby myself. I can wear it on my back in the woods, sleep less, quit drinking, and write while it naps. I will teach it what little I know. Electric pumps that fit the breast are used to stockpile mother's milk. Our freezer will be full of hard milk waiting for the thaw of an infant's scream.

We recently babysat a one-year-old girl as a dry run for our future. She slept on her side, arms and legs poised like a relief sculpture of a small running person. Upon awakening, she fouled her diaper with such vehemence that I actually gagged. I have seen men fill their veins with heroin. I've witnessed a limb-losing accident with a bulldozer, and the chilling aftermath of a gunshot wound. Nothing has ever quite roiled me like that diaper leaking around each chubby leg, obscuring genitals and streaking the belly. Rita calmly changed the baby, amused by my sensitivity.

Women are stronger, more ruthless in battle. Ancient Greeks feared even the ghosts of Amazon warriors, and built shrines to them for future control. Women invented language through application of sound to meaning. The earliest writings are by women, receipts for the sale of land in what is now Iraq. If childbearing were left to men, our species would have moldered because males could never accommodate the pain. We can barely get through hangovers and football games.

A kingfisher rattles its cry in midflight above the river. I watch it dive for a blue gill that is evading a larger fish by staying motionless just below the surface. The bird and the big fish attack the blue gill at the same moment. The big fish opens its mouth and the kingfisher stabs it through the palate. The bird is flipped into water and after a quick thrash, the big fish hauls it deep. A minute later the bird floats to the surface, still alive but so bewildered it is drowning. I know that scavengers will take the eyes first.

Humans have risen so fast that no one knows what's natural anymore. Rita works. I stay at home. She shops and cooks, I chop wood and take care of the car. She is a professional and I'm what's known as handy. We're not husband and wife, we're not our parents, and we're not some new breed of postmodern couple. We are a pair of mammals with a wide range of tolerance for each other.

The river flows at half-mast to mark the end of autumn. Dislodged leaves cover the seam of earth and water, blending the edges together. Paleolithic men considered women divine due to their inexplicable ability to create life. I know now that I've had a hand in it, but it doesn't make me feel much better. Routine activity betrayed the kingfisher, just as pregnancy is a breach of sex. I understand the bird's disbelief. I would trade my imagination for its wings.

The stillness of the desert at night pressed against every pore. In the inexplicable silence, I could hear blood coursing my veins, the steady rhythm of my heart like an oil derrick working without pause. I had no idea how hot it would be, how foolish my undertaking. After two days, my hair had paled and my skin was red. I'd bought a belt canteen but it was too small, only a quart. I decided to travel at night and sleep during the day, embedded in my sleeping bag, which turned wet and heavy from perspiration. At a diner I stole packets of salt and began eating it raw to replace my sweat.

Rides were few but they were usually very long. People drove at incredible speeds. Many carried water, a rifle, shovel, and CB radio. Two drivers referred to me as vulture bait. One told me the best place to sleep was on the sunset side of the huge red stones that poked from the land like petrified monsters. Afternoon heat, he said, was ten degrees warmer than the morning, a difference that could kill you sooner.

After three days of moving past dry lake beds, I traversed the Tehachapi Pass and began a descent, finally meandering north through the San Joaquin Valley. I woke from a nap in a ditch. With no clouds or pollution, the sun seemed to glow from the earth. Birdsong flowed through the air like a waterfall. I lay on my back and chewed a weed, watching bees tip blurred wings to my friendly flag. We were allies against the heat just beginning its afternoon grind. A ride was not important.

I dozed until a car rattled onto the shoulder, a dirty white coupe, scuffed at the corners. My mind groped the curious state between sleep and vigilance that stained reality like a minor hallucination. The driver's gray face was puffy as old dough. He hid a bald pate with long strands combed across his head in thin black lines. Heavy spectacles magnified his eyes. I got into the car and asked why he'd stopped.

"God's will!" he said. "You look harmless, that's all."

Road saviors were a common ride, the pious doing their duty to the downtrodden. The driver gave me long looks of appraisal before getting down to business: Was I a spiritually enlightened young man, or what? I mentioned a fault or two, admitted to confusion and the need for improvement. This standard patter encouraged a driver to discuss his faith. The devout were good for meals, but first the claptrap, as predictable as diarrhea. Occasionally they gave me money.

Al was a missionary who'd been questing after the ideal outpost for years, discarding each for various reasons. Some communities were so downright evil he'd be over his head. Others were too clean, better suited to a novice. Al was most frustrated by the places that contained a rival mission.

"It's there waiting for me. Maybe today. You will be with me, Chris. Think of that! It's God's will that we are brought together this day."

I asked what had started his expedition.

"Why, Armageddon of course! The prophecies are being fulfilled, my friend. Men and women live unmarried and sex is on TV. Grocery stores have electric machines that read invisible numbers. The Antichrist lives in Nevada."

"Are you scared, Al?"

"Of course not!" he shouted. "I am saved. I just want to live long enough to see the Lord burn the sinners where they stand. Then he will take the rest of us to heaven. I pray it happens before I die so my neighbors will know I'm not a sinner. People who are already dead get taken straight from the grave and nobody knows if they're sinners. But when Armageddon comes and you're alive, everybody can see!"

He pounded the road atlas between us, then brandished it like a warrior's shield. We were moving north through dense groves of citrus. The air held a sweet tang.

"Adam and Eve were the downfall and it was Eve's fault. She was weak and that's why all women are weak. They can't help it. You should learn from Adam's lesson not to pay attention to women. See what happened with Eve!"

"Uh, what, Al?"

"Sex, sickness, and insects."

"Insects?"

Solemn now, he licked saliva from his lips. Wind snapped his hair like a metronome.

"Heaven has no insects! All flowers and no smog. Fresh fruits and vegetables. A paradise! Everything so pure that our body can digest seeds, stem, and core. That way there's no urination or defecation. No need for toilets at all. Think of that!"

I asked about the devil, and Al babbled for miles about his habits. Once a man knew God, old Lucifer worked on him extra, singling him out for special attention. A simple bedtime prayer drew the devil quick as a gnat. He'd make paint fall off your house and send you drunken workmen. You'd cut yourself shaving every morning if you didn't pray first. He showed me proof—a network of tiny white scars the size of ringworms on his neck.

According to Al, insects were Satan's private little terrorist force. The Garden was bugless until Eve screwed up, but now the devil dispensed bee stings and mosquito bites. Flies fornicated on the formica. The day Al converted, a band of termites chewed his attic rafters in half and dropped the roof around the chimney. As a countermove, he began raising spiders.

"They eat insects like candy. I got some pedigreed for six generations. The good ones are in the back seat."

I peeked in the back. Nestled among frayed religious tracts were several jars. I stared out the window at the fruit trees, smelling lemon scent mingled with manure. Streaks of sky peeked through the gray haze. I studied the map and asked him to drop me off at the San Joaquin River a few miles away.

"After Armageddon," he said, "the earth will be smoky and black! Great chunks of landscape burnt to cinders. Every insect killed. God, my friend, is like a giant exterminator sparing only spiders and Christians. Think of that!"

"What about survivors, Al?"

"None! I don't mean to scare you, Chris, but God won't give sinners a break!"

At the river Al asked me to pray with him. We bowed our heads to the dashboard. Frayed stuffing leaked through a crack in the plastic.

"It's me, God. Your servant, Al. I want to ask my favor of the week. Give this young man a ride. Let him wait no longer than five minutes. And one more thing, God. Please bring Armageddon as fast as you can. I beseech you to bring it before I die. Now is fine, Lord. Amen."

I left the car, surprised by his humdinger of a prayer. Al reached into a cardboard box and passed me a small jar containing a pure-bred spider. Breathing holes were punched through the metal lid.

"Thanks," I said.

"Don't trust men who smoke a pipe."

He ground the gears of the old three-on-the-tree and lurched along the highway. The white car scudded into the quivering heat lines and disappeared around a bend. I opened the jar in the dusty grass. The spider walked to the edge and poked a leg out. It faced the world for a few seconds before crawling back into the safety of its glass chapel.

Quite suddenly I was alone with the land, out of the valley and against the river. Shadows darkened the trees as the air cooled. My hackles went higher than a cat's back. Early crickets sounded ominous, like warning sirens. A muddy feeling in my skin sent me reeling, jerking my head in all directions. Insects were everywhere.

Exactly five minutes later a rental truck spewed gravel on the shoulder and veered to a stop. The orange door bounced open, disgorging a bearded giant dressed in black. He wore a leather vest over a T-shirt emblazoned with a faded American flag; a towering silhouette with the voice of a rusty rake.

"Where you headed for, boy?"

"North."

"Drive a truck?"

At my nod he spun like a soldier and clambered into the cab. I followed. He cursed, gauged my reaction, and cursed again as introduction.

"My name's Chris."

"Wi'er."

"Like winter and summer?"

"Like loser."

A fence flowed by the window, tracking my attention. I should have kept the spider. A few miles later Winner cursed and spoke.

"Awake two days straight since getting laid."

"Mmmm."

"In the backyard on a picnic table. Preacher's daughter." Winner laughed, a chain saw hitting an embedded spike. "Had to strap a two-by-four across my back to keep from falling in. She worked my kickstand all night long."

Winner had left at dawn with a half-gram of crystal Methedrine that was beginning to wear off after thirty-eight hours.

"What're we hauling?" I said.

"My scooter. Going home to take care of Mama. Scooter took a fall same day she broke her hip. Have to leave this truck outside of town and ride in. Won't look right me coming home in a truck. Got to be on my scooter."

"Sure, Winner. Just like I got to be on my thumb."

His grin exposed battered teeth. "Ya fucking A!" he screamed, and backhanded me across the chest.

As I struggled to breathe, Winner withdrew a revolver from under the seat and fired out the window. The sound roared against my ears. He winked at me, kissed the shiny wooden grip, and tucked the gun away. The truck cab stank of cordite. Sweat trickled down my sides and I took long, careful breaths. The pistol shot had ignited the final flecks of speed twitching through his body. An extended monologue ensued, difficult to follow at times, littered with laughter and an occasional backhand to my chest. When I saw one coming, I exhaled ahead of impact.

For the past six years Winner had been "in the field" packing grease-soaked weapons in aluminum boxes. Some caches were in caves, others down a well, or simply buried. All over the nation, guns and ammunition lay snuggled in the earth awaiting World War III. Winner was one of many soldiers laying siege to an awful future. He reported the sites to his superiors twice a year, once in Ohio and again in a bayou town of Louisiana.

"We got gasoline and water, food and weapons," he said. "They don't fuck with a machine gun!"

"Who, Winner?"

"The commie pricks and mutants, that's who! If you got food and water, everybody will want it. The mutants first because the commie pricks will be a while getting here. They got to wait for things to settle down. It'll be messy the first couple of years."

"But not you."

"Ya fucking A! I'm a patriot. I'll have my gas mask and M-16. On the lookout."

"For commies?"

"For women!" he roared, belting my chest.

Winner launched into an anticommunist diatribe that encircled the globe. Every country was in cahoots against us. They wanted our money, our women, and our motorcycles. Any day we'd be maced by a few hundred rockets, a flock of lethal birds flying west for a long winter. Only scooter shops and girls' schools would be spared.

"They're smarter than us, the fucks. The enemy always is. You got to think that way, see. They'll nail us first, and only one place will be safe."

"Kentucky?"

"Shit no! They'll crack Fort Knox like busting a rubber. The only state that won't be full of fallout is Idaho. Experts figured it out.

And Idaho," he dropped his voice to a ragged whisper. "Idaho is the mother-hole. We got guys there all the time. A city underground."

"Just getting ready?"

"Ya fucking A! You wanna be a mutant with half a face and green hair. Your kids born blind with no pecker. Living like pigs. It won't be me!" Winner caressed the knife at his hip. "See this blade, brother. It's a hollow handle. Inside I got me a couple of Liberation Pills for radiation. If I'm shit creek, all I gotta do is pop them. No shame if your skin's falling off. Nothing wrong with dying, it's all in how you go. Battle's best because when you die strong, you're stronger in your next life. If you go pansy, you come back worse. It's a proven fact. Scientists did it. You got to be ready all the time because they might hit today. We won't know till it's too late, but they better fucking wait until I see Mama!"

"Uh, Winner. Who all's in on this?"

"There's me and my brothers for starts. Back east it's all farmers. What the fuck are you so nosy for?"

"Maybe you got room for an extra man."

His right arm snaked across the seat and grabbed my chin. His thumb pressed my jaw while his fingers sank into my cheek. He jerked my head, squinting at me.

"What's your last name?" he said.

I told him.

"And your mother's?"

"McCabe."

"You willing to swear on the flag and Bible you're solid white? Not a drop of nigger, kike, Mex, A-rab, wop, or Indian in you?"

I nodded until my head hurt and my jaw felt like it was cracking. He released me.

"Sorry, boy," he said, "but that's what it's all about."

"What?"

"Us."

That remains the most frightening word I've heard uttered in a lifetime of conversation with strangers. Epithets could be dodged, scatology shrugged off. But "us" was chilling. Us meant lynch mobs and gang rape, book burning and genocide. Us was a synonym for control, the grim satisfaction of veracity reflected in a corroded mirror. "Us" implied a "them," and all thems were ripe for destruction. Aristotle set the precedent: "There are Greeks and there are slaves."

As suddenly as he had begun, Winner was silent. The amphetamines darted away, stilling his tongue, making him slouch. We were high in the mountains. Clouds piled each other for miles, bellies tinted scarlet by the setting sun. The air turned purple to the east.

"Mutants, spies, and commies." Winner muttered. "Shoot on sight. Burn the carcass. Stay upwind."

"Yup."

"Ya fucking A! They got satellites to take a picture a thousand miles up. See every hair on your ass."

The meth had shot its wad. Winner steered to the shoulder and we switched sides. In less than a minute he slept the speed freak's twitchy sleep and I studied the tattoos on his arms. An eyeball topped a pyramid sitting on a skull. Spiderwebs stretched between his knuckles. The number thirteen crinkled at the base of his thumb. Etched into flesh was the phrase "Born Dead."

I leaned out the window, allowing the wind to scrub my face. Stars sprinkled the night sky like a random computer printout. A full moon hugged the mountains. Bug corpses smeared the windshield, reminding me of Al. Maybe he and Winner were both correct—the world was doomed to extinction. Global annihilation was better than getting old; heaven and reincarnation were the same guarantee. No one surfed the river Styx.

Winner dropped me off at dawn near a town called French Gulch and I followed Highway 299 west to the coast. For a week I wandered down the edge of what Spanish explorers originally considered to be an island. Years later wagon trains lost everything on their western trips, following ruts six feet deep. The desert fried the very old and the very young. Spring settlers passed thawing corpses. Now there are seventy languages spoken in Los Angeles and if California were a country, it would be the sixth most productive in the world. The state was like the end of a pier crowded by fishermen with tangled lines, all hoping for a big one.

The first night, I slept on the beach. My backpack was stolen by two kids on bicycles. I went to a homeless shelter, where row after row of cots lined a stained floor. To prevent theft while sleeping, I threaded one arm through my jacket and rolled up the rest of my clothes for a pillow. Instead of camaraderie with my brothers, I felt like a pariah invading their ranks. These guys were hard-luck, hard-bit men, not like me at all. The shelter held men who tricked at night and saved their money for a sex change, men who spat tubercular blood, men who'd lost their apartments to co-op renovators, their jobs to automation.

All of us denied that we were truly homeless. Every conversation began with past success, then skipped to the future. The present was never mentioned. We were living in a temporary situation, each believing our own was more temporary than the rest. Cigarettes were currency. Talk was defense. I babbled constantly and the creeps left me alone.

I spent my days at the beach, eating tacos and staring at women in slight swimsuits. They trimmed their yoni hair in order to expose more flesh. No one looked at me. I was invisible, a nonentity. I craved every woman who walked by, but understood that there was nothing for me save fantasy. Twice I was run off particular sections of sand by surfers.

I began drawing, signing and dating each sketch, and leaving them in front of the scene I'd sketched. I imagined that an art dealer was tracking my passage, saving every drawing. He'd eventually contact me with an offer of studio space and supplies if I'd translate my brilliant studies into paintings. In the meantime, my journal entries evolved into prolonged arguments against writing and in favor of the visual arts, efforts to convince myself that drawing was a stronger medium than writing. Eventually art won my private feud. I'd successfully used language to talk myself out of using it.

I watched a man discover one of my sketches tucked between the redwood boards of a picnic table. He was well dressed and carried a briefcase. I moved close to him, waiting for recognition. He wadded the paper and dropped it in a garbage can.

"Hey," I said. "That's mine. I drew that."

"Jesus," he said. "Now I'll have to wash my fucking hands. You bums are bad enough without leaving your trash around."

My perception of myself underwent an abrupt seismic shift: I slept in a homeless shelter and told stories to myself. I stole paper and pencil to leave my mark. No one knew me, or knew where I was. I suddenly understood that mortality was trivial. I felt dizzy, shaken to the marrow. A stranger considered me litter that produced further litter. I vowed never to draw again. I'd become a playwright. It would be easy. Plays were nothing but talk, and I'd write down every word I overheard, then weld them together. My entire life had led to this decision. At land's edge, I'd found my true ambition.

California, however, was the wrong place to begin my new career and I left the coast the following morning. On the bus to the edge of town I filled three pages with conversational scraps overheard from nearby seats. These notes would form the basis for my first work, a one-act play about riding a bus. I was on the move again. I had a plan. The future was golden.

There is no sun today, only a gray light filtered through the gauze of air. Leafless trees cage the sky. A smattering of snow has dusted the ground, a flurry that lingered. It is enough to transform the woods. The temperature has risen to nineteen and the heat has drawn birds into the boughs of trees. The titmouse is the bravest, the wren the most cheerful. Oddly, the small creatures allow me greater proximity before flight. The large ones—deer, fox, the bears from home—all flee at my approach. The same is true of humanity. When we are small, we let others in close, then begin the gradual pushing away that so often leaves the very old utterly alone.

There is an ancient maple in the woods, long dead but still upright, with a trunk the size of a small car. The tree is rotted, its guts hollow. At the base is an opening big enough to enter. I have taken to sitting inside this tree. No one knows I do this.

I am heading for the maple when my nose finds a scent before my eyes see the cause. It's the sweetly nauseating smell that, once learned, is always known. I sniff in every direction and gauge the wind. The smell is to the west. I move that way. Animal tracks lead to the site in weaving lines that remind me of the layout of a web. At its center is a mound of clear plastic bags, several of which have been torn open. They are freezer bags containing the skinned carcasses of small game. The work is very precise. Every leg bears a neat cut above the ankle that leaves the paw still furry. Each animal appears to be wearing slippers. A hairless tail lies in the snow like a snake. I remember having read that one percent of all human newborns possess a tiny tail that is quickly clipped and thrown away.

A shift of wind pushes the smell against me and I have the sense of it clinging to my face. The nearest frosty bag resembles an amnion holding a fetus. I walk rapidly away. Half of all pregnancies do not make it to term and sometimes the fetus will die late in the womb, during the second or third trimester. Labor is then induced. The woman endures it, knowing in advance that she is giving birth to a baby already dead.

I stop walking, sick to my stomach, angry at myself for thinking this way, for not being able to dispel the image from my mind. A pale horizontal band shimmers at waist level everywhere I look. When I concentrate on seeing it, the stripe goes away. Curiosity replaces the nausea, and I wonder if I've become too isolated, have spent too much time alone in the woods. As I ponder this, the stripe returns. It's not in the air but on the tree trunks. My eyes have merely supplied the band's continuance through empty space. Up close, the mark is faint, nearly invisible, a stain on the bark. When I hold my eyes steady and turn my head, I see the line very clearly on all the trees. It is the high-water mark from last spring's flood.

At the hollow maple, I crouch and crawl inside. Light enters from above, where the fork has split and fallen away. The first time I came in, there were animal prints, but the awful presence of man is enough to keep intruders away. I sit on my haunches like old men at home, weight on my heels, each elbow on a knee. The inner bark of the tree is as desiccated as the dry river mud of summer. From here I can peer into the woods unseen. A woodpecker works a tree nearby, blinking each time its beak strikes wood. If it didn't, the impact would drive the eyes from its skull.

There is a subtle difference between feeling lonely—that inner peril of the mind—and the simple lack of company that makes me lonesome. Rita takes the edge off both. Perhaps the baby will cut the loneliness further, make me need the woods less. I realize that I'm thinking backwards, that it is the kid who will rely on me. It may never be a friend.

Gunshots echo from across the river, a hunter sighting on a deer. Carrying a weapon into the woods transforms perceptions; one is no longer on equitable ground, sharing time and space. The spear of the necessary hunt has given way to the rifle of sport. I've eaten the forbidden possum, snake, coon, and horse, as well as rabbit, squirrel, and deer. All bounty of the woods is welcome at my door. These days, however, I prefer my liaison with nature to be one of peace.

Taking life is as biologically grounded as giving life. Every animal kills to live. Eating fruit, vegetables, and grain is no escape; plants are living things. They have gender and home, suffer when hurt, and attempt to heal themselves. Tree stumps sprout each year, offspring produced by roots still sucking water. I believe that like an amputee whose missing limb aches, the tree knows when a branch is gone.

Leaving the maple is more difficult than entering. I lie on my back, brace my boots against the inner walls, and push myself faceup into the woods. The woodpecker cocks its head and looks at me. When I stand, it flits away, scalloping the air with its telltale flight.

I carefully skirt the pile of animals, then decide against retreat. A father must face everything. I try to open my vision in the way that helped me see the watermark on the trees. I think of the woodpeckers that must have blinded themselves before the species learned to blink.

Live game are using the dead for food, and it occurs to me that this is not a mass grave, or an omen of miscarriage. It is simply the residue of older ways. A trapper has cleared out his freezer for better fare, perhaps a deer. Prairie winters are harsh and he is helping the animals to survive. The pelts gave cash to the trapper, the deer gave him food, and he has returned the favor of the woods. In our own way, Rita and I are engaged in a similar cycle, giving ourselves to the world. After the baby is born, stages of childhood will replace seasons for charting time.

I look back at the hollow maple and nod my head once, glad that no one is here to witness this. I walk out of the woods, my tracks bisecting animal trails in strange geometry. Behind me the woodpecker labors for larvae to survive the season. Ahead, Rita is waiting, very calmly, waiting. She has her own high-water mark to watch. Soon the snow will fly, the color of salt, the smell of life.

Allowing oneself to sleep in rain is the mark of a soldier, an animal, and the consummate hitchhiker. It was a skill I never fully acquired. Water weight trebled the mass of my pack. Rain gathered in my brows and ran into my eyes at the slightest movement. There is a private understanding, even appreciation, of misery when one is cold and wet at four in the morning. Dawn never seemed so precious. Birdsong meant that soon you could watch the rising steam drawn from your clothes by sun. In this fashion, I began a summer in Alabama.

The sun hung low on the horizon when the leader of a convoy came traveling my way. Emblazoned along the truck in red curlicued letters were the words "Hendley Circus, Greatest Show on Earth." Truck after truck passed, each garishly advertising various sideshows. Horse droppings spilled from a trailer. A variety of campers and RVs followed, but none stopped and no one waved. The last vehicle trundled from sight and I felt as though I'd seen a mirage, a phantom wagon train that taunted hermits of the road.

From the west came the sound of another truck straining in low gear. The driver flung open the passenger door without stopping.

"Hurry," he said. "I can't stop or Peaches will get mad."

I used the mirror to vault onto the running board, and scrambled into the seat.

"Thanks," I said.

"No problem. I've been on the run plenty."

"It's not like that."

"It never is," he said. "You got five bucks to loan me?"

"I'm broke."

He slid a hand into his shirt pocket and handed me a five-dollar bill. He spat tobacco juice out the window.

"Little treat for Peaches," he said. "She loves 'backer."

"Who's Peaches?"

"My best friend of fifteen years. The circus is my mistress but Peaches is my wife."

The way the truck swayed at low speed, I figured he was married to the sideshow Fat Lady, who wouldn't fit up front. If he wanted to haul his wife in the back, it was his business.

Barney had been in the circus all his life, a case of "sawdust up my nose when I was a little pecker." He offered me a job, saying that I owed him a Lincoln already. Room and board were included in the wage. Four hours later we passed through a tiny town and joined the rest of the caravan, circled like a pioneer wagon train in a broad grassy vale. Barney hopped from the cab and handed me a rake.

"Clear the rocks from behind the truck, then make a path to the big top."

Barney climbed on the rear bumper and unhooked chains bigger than those used by professional loggers. He cranked down the gate, revealing the great gray flanks of an elephant. Barney spoke to Peaches in a soothing tone, apologizing for the long trip, offering her water and hay if she'd come out of the truck. A foot extended backwards. I scurried away so fast I fell. Raucous laughter erupted behind me.

"What a fall, what a fall! Sign him up!"

"Move over, Rover, he's mashing clover!"

A pair of dwarfs leered from giant heads on neckless bodies. One performed a handspring, then clambered onto the shoulders of his buddy. They advanced on me, my size now, flicking their tongues like snakes. I held the rake across my body.

"Rover's got a rake," said one.

"Let's throw him in the lake."

"There ain't no lake."

"How about a well?"

"That sounds good."

The top dwarf kicked the lower one in the head.

"Swell," the top one said. "You should have said swell for the rhyme."

"Don't kick me."

The lower dwarf bit his partner's ankle and they tumbled across the ground. Peaches aimed her trunk high, bellowing relief at standing on earth. Barney stepped around her with a long pole that ended in a hook.

"Hey, you fricking runts," he yelled. "Peaches favors tidbits like you."

The dwarfs scrambled away, hopping onto the metal steps of a camper.

"I'll make a suitcase out of her," one said.

"Planters from her feet."

"A dildo of her trunk."

Peaches regarded me from an eye the size of my fist. Thick stalks of hair poked from her body like weed clumps. Her back leg held a heavy manacle that chained her to the truck.

"Stay away from them shrimps," Barney said. "Watch out for the clowns, too. And don't even look at the Parrot Lady. Even from behind. She can tell."

I nodded, receiving information without the ability to process it.

"Go to the trucks and ask for Flathead. Tell him you're my First of May."

I moved across the field, listening to yelling and cursing everywhere. No one talked in normal tones. People were setting up sideshow games, running electric wires, unloading animals. A vast crew of men worked four trucks loaded with folded tents. Flathead's curly hair was very short, as if to display the fact that his head was indeed flat on top. He told me to dig a donicker.

"What?"

"The donicker hole. What's the matter, you no piss? Everybody piss. Dig two hole, you."

He handed me a shovel and sent me to an area at the edge of the campers. Everyone ignored me. I finished my work and walked away. A man strode past me and calmly urinated into the hole.

I returned to Flathead, who sent me to a canvas crew that was short a pair of hands. Trucks circled the field, stopping at precise points aligned with iron stakes driven into the ground. Several men dragged the folded sections of tent from the back of the truck. I was a runner. When pulled fast, canvas becomes slightly airborne, not so heavy, and easier to handle. Another man and I held a corner of the canvas and ran as hard as we could to the extent of the fold, went back, grabbed the next corner and ran again. The canvas sandpapered my hands to blood.

When the sections were laid out, we laced them together while the more experienced men fastened the canvas to bail rings. Walking on the tent risked tearing it, so everyone crawled like bugs, even Flathead. Next came the complicated process of raising the top, one section at a time, to keep them even. My chore was to hold a guy line until Flathead yelled to tie it off. It reminded me of water-skiing—incredible exertion while standing still.

After nine hours, Peaches hoisted the final pole with ropes tied to her harness. The entire tent strained upward while everyone watched, feeling the increased tension in the lines. Flathead tied off the main pole. In the dim interior, we set up three tiers of collapsible bleachers, cursed by electricians and sound people. Flathead announced we were finished and everyone began asking if the flag was up. We staggered into an afternoon sunlight so brilliant we bumped against each other. The entire mass of exhausted men hurried away and I trailed behind, following the herd. Since I hadn't understood that an upright flag meant dinner was served, I was late. The only thing worse than the dregs of the stew was knowing that everyone else's sweat had fallen into the pot.

A cook sent me to the sleeper truck for canvas boys. Four levels of bunk beds lined each wall, with a thin corridor running the length of the truck. Our collective bedroom was a mobile lightless hall, extremely hot, that reeked of unwashed bodies. Snoring echoed back and forth between the metal walls. I found an empty bunk and lay on a mattress the width of a bookshelf.

We stayed three days in town, long enough for me to prove myself a fierce liability as a taffy seller. The candy was cut into tiny plugs that could pull fillings from a molar. I was unable to hawk it aggressively enough to please the head of concessions, a bitter man who limped. He'd been an aerialist until a fall ruined his ankle. His performing monicker had been Colonel Kite but everyone called him Colonel Corn. After my dismal failure as a candy seller, he decided he liked me since I was less suited to employment than he was. The Colonel rather graciously gave me the lowest job of folding waxed paper around the candy.

The circus possessed a hierarchy with the complex simplicity of the military. Those who rode horses in a standing position were on top of the heap, followed by aerialists, live animal performers, clowns, and the ringmaster. Sideshow freaks made up the middle level. Everyone else drifted at the bottom, producing their own pecking order based on convincing their peers of personal prowess. Canvas boys were the lowest. We had no one to despise but minorities and homosexuals. Since circus people hated them already, the canvas boys were left with honing bigotry to a fine edge.

The technicians seemed to have the simplest job, and I approached Krain, the light man, about work. He led me up a precarious ladder to the booth. Protruding from slots in a metal board were several levers that controlled the intensity of the lights. Krain pulled an electrical wire from beneath the board, separated the two strands, and tucked each one in his jaws, clamped between his teeth. He gradually pushed the lever forward. His eyes got very wide and his lips pulled back in a macabre grin. At quarter power, his head and shoulders began quivering. He brought it back to the zero mark, calmly pulled the wires from his mouth, and offered them to me. I climbed down the ladder.

The aerialists and horse performers never deigned to speak with anyone. As Europeans, they considered themselves superior to the rest of us. The two clowns were hilarious in performance, making me laugh long after I knew their gags. On the occasional free day, they went fishing. I followed them once, hoping for some intangible insight into the private world of professional clowns. I watched from the bushes. They carried tackle boxes and baited their hooks like normal men. They cast and reeled and did not converse. When one caught a fish, the other nodded. The only shift from standard behavior was their method of removing a fish from the line. With a ferocious motion, they ripped the hook free, usually trailing bits of the fish's interior. Often it was bleeding from the gills.

No one liked the dwarfs because they made more money than anyone else, and in violation of circus tradition, they didn't squander the loot. At each new town they inquired after the stock market.

In addition to Peaches, the circus boasted three bedraggled tigers that reared on their hind legs as if begging, perched on stools, and crowded together on a large box. A man dressed as a woman snapped the whip over their striped flanks. I was leery of him until the Colonel explained his clothing—an audience was more awed by a female tamer than a male. The tiger man's great enemy, due to her withering disdain, was the Parrot Lady. The dwarfs called her "an upper crustacean."

She was part of a sideshow that included a perpetually drunk magician, a trained walrus, and a skinny man, double-jointed at every junction, who could fold himself into knots. There was a strong man who was dying from steroid intake. His brother was a fire eater who told me the hardest part was controlling a sneeze.

The most popular act was the Parrot Lady. She'd begun as a common sword swallower, but like everyone, had wanted to increase her earnings by diversifying her act. Five years later she was the biggest sideshow draw. Women and children were not allowed in her tent. The huge MEN ONLY sign fostered quite a crowd, and on slow nights, teenage boys were admitted for double the price. I watched her performance every night. The tent was always packed, hot, and hazed by cigarette smoke.

She entered from stage left wearing a high-necked, long-sleeved, white formal gown, looking like an aristocrat. The audience gradually hushed beneath her unwavering stare. After a long spell of silence, she began speaking in a voice so low that everyone strained to hear. Each night she told the dirtiest joke imaginable, speaking of cocks, cunts, and fucking as casually as the men's wives might discuss children and meals. A palpable sense of guilt congealed with lust in the tent, and the men refused to look at one another.

The Parrot Lady stood very still. Her eyes fluttered to stage right and she lifted a hand to her ear. Faint chamber music drifted through the tent. With the grace of a fashion model, she rose from her stool and began an excruciatingly slow strip—from the inside out. She removed a slip first, a petticoat, her shoes, stockings, and two more petticoats, each frillier than the last. She took off her bra and panties last. No one moved. Everyone knew she was naked beneath the dress, a fact more arresting than if she'd actually been nude.

She faced the audience and began to unbutton her dress, beginning at the top of the chin-high collar and working down. Holding the front closed, she continued to her lower belly. The men were leaning forward without awareness of their posture. When her arms could no longer reach the buttons, she turned her back. The long train concealed her legs. Nothing was visible except her slightly bowed head and the long dress that everyone knew was open in front. She remained standing this way a long time. Instead of building to a crescendo, the music faded to silence. The spotlight narrowed its focus. She let the dress fall from her shoulders. Breath came pouring from the men as if each had received a powerful blow in the guts.

Tattoos of brilliant tropical birds covered every inch of her body. Two parrots faced each other on her buttocks, beaks curving into the cleft, tail feathers running down the back of her legs. A swirling flock of bright plumage fluttered up her back and across her shoulders. Parakeets perched among toucans and birds of paradise. Lush jungle foliage peeped around the birds.

Slowly she turned, revealing a shaven yoni from which a pair of golden wings fanned along her hips. On top of each breast sat two enormous and lovely parrots. She rotated again, moving at a slow pace until she faced the men once more. She now held a long fluorescent light tube. An electric cord ran behind the black curtain. She spread her legs for balance and tipped her head back. Only her neck and the point of her chin were visible. She lifted the light tube above her head and very slowly slid it down her throat. She took her hands away, and pressed a switch on the cord that turned on the fluorescent tube. The spotlight went black. Her body glowed from within, illuminating the birds in an ethereal, ghostly light, like a jungle dawn. She flicked the switch off and the tent was dark save for sunlight leaking beneath the canvas flaps. The houselights came on very bright. The stage was empty. She was gone.

The dazed men stumbled outside, blinking against the sun. I never missed her act and always tried to maneuver myself near the front. After ten or twelve shows, I was sufficiently familiar with the birds to begin watching her eyes. I expected a blank look but she gazed at the men with a blend of fury and desire. Eventually she saw me watching. I was embarrassed, as if caught peeping, a curious reverse of logic. The following day I stayed in the back but she found me. Her vision locked on me during the entire act. I left with the crowd, feeling devastated.

My tear-down job was pulling stakes, a chore relegated to the most useless worker. The stakes were car axles driven very deep into the earth. To pull them, I first had to loosen the dirt by pounding the ground with a sledgehammer. At times I worked in a rhythmic blur, grateful for the simple repetition. Other times I wore myself down in rage at my occupation.

I abandoned my bunk after a wave of lice spread among the workers, making us scratch like junkies. If our hands were full, we wiggled and shifted in vain attempts to relieve the itch. I boiled my clothes and the sight of swollen nits in the seams made me sick. Since I was being fed and housed, my pay was not enough to buy new clothes. When my toothbrush snapped at the handle, I decided to quit.

I told Barney, who said he'd speak to Flathead about my working as an all-purpose animal helper. For the next two weeks we traveled across the Deep South. In many of the smaller towns attendance at the circus included a black night and a white night. The Sunday matinees were the only integrated time, but the groups didn't mix. I swept manure, hauled feed and water, and hosed down Peaches twice a day. Barney lent me money against my raise. I bought clothes and a toothbrush. Luckily, I'd been keeping my journal in the glove box of Barney's pickup. Everything else had been stolen from the sleeper truck.

The new job gave me greater privacy. I slept under the truck and had time to write in my journal. I never reread an entry. They represented the past, and my journal was proof that I existed in the present. As an event unfolded around me, I was already anticipating how I'd write about it later. A new entry began where the last one ended, continuing to the immediate, to the current act of writing. Each mark on the page was a gesture toward the future, a codification of the now. Through this, I learned to trust language.

The animal trainers were an odd lot who argued constantly, smoked hand-rolled cigarettes, and possessed only one friend apiece—their animal. Soon I began to roll my own cigarettes. During off-hours we sat in a circle debating the merits and dangers of various animals. Everyone teased Arnie, the gorilla trainer, about the simplicity of his job. Gabe the Gorilla was ancient and nearly blind.

One night the show was canceled due to a fire in town that destroyed four blocks. The entire circus left except the trainers who stayed to guard their animals. We passed a pint of whisky and began our usual bickering.

"Don't go getting the big head, Barney," the tiger man said. "Elephant ain't the worst to work."

"More of mine kill folks than yours ever did," Barney said.

"Killing ain't the mark," the man said. "Go a season with zebras and you'll wish you had a rogue. Zebras is the meanest there is."

"Bull smoke," said Arnie.

"Fact before God. Over in Africa the zebra's worst enemy is a lion. That makes them a mean fighter."

The others pushed a lower lip out and raised their eyebrows in the animal trainer's sign of acknowledgment.

"My opinion," the horse man said, "the all-time worstest is a camel. I purely loathe a camel. There ain't no safe place to work them from because they kick sideways. I never seen a sideways kick that didn't bust a leg to a compound. Humpy bastards are stubborn as a mule."

Barney drank from the bottle as it went past him.

"The elephant is the closest animal to a man there is," he said.

"Bull smoke," said Arnie.

"Telling it true," Barney said. "Its back legs bends forward like a human. They got tits up front, not in the back. They go off on their own to mate."

"Gorilla's ten times closer to human," Arnie said.

"Well, a cat ain't," said the tiger man. "I'm put right out of this talk. The only thing a cat's like is a damn cat."

"Horse is gabbier," the horse man said.

"Bull smoke," Arnie said. "Me and Gabe talk plenty."

"I heard something on a gorilla maybe you can clear up," Barney said. "But I ain't advising you to ask Gabe on it."

"What?"

"A gorilla's got a harem, don't it?"

Arnie nodded. "In the wild."

"Then it don't have to work too hard for company, if you know what I mean." Barney tipped his head to me. "I'm trying to talk nice in front of the squirt."

Everyone laughed and the tiger man handed me the bottle. "That boy knows what's what," he said. "He ain't missed the Parrot Lady since he joined on." The men chuckled again.

"Way I hear it," Barney said, "the gorilla's got the littlest balls of any creature on earth. They shrink up from not having to hunt no nookie."

"Bull smoke," Arnie said. "They're big as a man's."

"Damn cat's got his snuggled up to his butt-hole," the tiger man said. "I got to find me another animal to work if I want to keep up with this outfit."

"Is that true?" the horse man said. "About the gorilla?"

"No," Arnie said. "Gabe's balls are big as mine."

"That ain't saying much." Barney grinned at the men. "We might just have to get some proof on that."

"We got eighty proof right here," the tiger man said.

He opened another pint of local rotgut, took a hard drink, and sent it on its rounds.

"Might be tough to see Gabe's balls," Barney said. "Little as they are."

"All you got to do is get him to stand," Arnie said. "We can squat low and put a flashlight on him. They're a good size, you can take my word for it."

"Chris, there's a flashlight behind the truck seat. Get the elephant prod, too."

I walked through the warm summer darkness, rummaged for the light, and returned. The men were swaying on their feet.

"Gabe ain't going to like this much," Arnie said.

"He won't know," the horse man said.

"He will. He's smarter than any nag you run."

"All right," Barney said. "We'll make it so Gabe don't know what we're up to."

"Nobody better say nothing," Arnie said. "Promise?"

"Deal," Barney said.

The men nodded. We walked to the gorilla cage, which was

bolted to a flatbed truck. Arnie fastened a banana to the end of the elephant prod.

"Gabe," he whispered. "You awake in there."

Gabe's tiny close-set eyes showed red in the flashlight's beam. Arnie waved the banana. "You hungry? I sneaked you a snack." He lifted the elephant prod until the banana was above the cage, just outside of the bars. "Come and get it, big boy."

Gabe moved to the front of the cage. We squatted for an up-angle view while Barney played the flashlight on Gabe's crotch. The gorilla used the bars to pull himself erect on legs that seemed permanently crooked. His big thighs were matted with fur.

"Up, Gabe," Arnie said. "You almost got it."

The gorilla stretched higher. He shifted his weight to one leg and reached his hand through the top of the cage, inches from the banana. He thrust his other leg out for balance. Clearly illuminated was a pair of testicles the size of chestnuts. The men collapsed on their haunches, laughing and hooting. Gabe quickly dropped to a crouch and backed into the shadows. The men laughed harder.

"Goddamn it!" Arnie yelled. "You promised to be quiet."

"You win," the horse man said. "By default."

He handed the bottle to Arnie, who knocked it aside. He snatched the flashlight and aimed the light through the bars. Gabe sat hunched in a corner, head bowed. He glanced at us with an expression of terrible humiliation, then hid his head. The men hushed and slowly moved away.

"You sons of bitches," Arnie said. "You promised!"

He continued cursing into the night until his voice broke and we heard a sob. He started talking to Gabe in low tones. I crawled under the elephant truck to sleep, remembering my former roommates' preoccupation with the heft of Marduk's lingam. Men's tendency to take an interest in one another's genitals is not so much sexual as simply wondering how they stack up against everybody else. Most men need confirmation that someone's equipment is smaller than theirs, even if it belongs to a gorilla.

After lunch, Flathead always strolled the grounds to ensure that everyone was ready for the afternoon show. Sometimes the clowns or the magician were so hung over they needed an injection of sucrose and Dexedrine. Flathead carried a small case of prepared syringes. That morning Gabe refused to eat breakfast, keeping his back turned in the cage. Flathead wanted to give him an injection but Arnie refused, promising to have his gorilla ready for the matinee. Gabe missed both performances and Flathead was furious. If Gabe didn't perk up, Flathead warned, they'd sell him to a Mexican zoo.

The animal trainers avoided each other all day. They took care of the animals and went to sleep without talking. Sometime late in the night, Barney woke me by rapping on my feet. The trainers stood in an awkward circle. The horse man pushed his shoes against the earth while the tiger man paced back and forth. Barney was very still and Arnie stood by himself, facing away.

Barney handed each of us a banana. He stepped to the gorilla cage and held the flashlight so that it shone on his face.

"I'm sorry, Gabe," he said. "I was a little drunk. When I was married, I cheated on my wife. Now you know something on me."

He peeled the banana and gently slid it into the cage. One by one, each of us took our turn apologizing to Gabe, who sat motionless in the shadows. Everyone told him something personal and gave him a banana. On my turn I faced the darkness and muttered my greatest secret—the transvestite in New York. Gabe didn't answer.

Arnie went last. He was crying. He opened his pants and said, "See, they ain't that much to mine either." Arnie stuffed four bananas through the cage and claimed credit for bringing all the men to apologize.

We slipped away, leaving them to talk in private. The next day, Gabe performed exceedingly well. After the show, the trainers sat in their customary circle, arguing the fine points of manure, each defending his animal.

The circus roamed deeper into the South and I was rewarded for my diligence with a promotion that, like most advances I've received, proved my undoing. Someone had quit and Flathead offered me the job because of my size—the circus diet and strenuous labor had cost me several pounds. I was practically a wraith. Flathead introduced me to Mr. Kaybach, a dirty-haired man whose odor was a point of personal honor. As long as I stayed upwind, we got along well.

He showed me how to wriggle into my costume, an oilskin sheath with a hidden zipper. He warned that it was hot and I should wear only underwear. Tattered quilting padded the interior to swell my torso. Two flippers hung from my chest which I could operate by careful insertion of my hands. The back of the costume tapered to a pair of rubber flippers set close together. A surprisingly realistic mask completed my transformation into a walrus. I peeked through tiny slits between two tusks. Kaybach explained our routine and I waited eagerly inside the dark tent for my debut.

The audience encircled a pool of water containing fake ice floes and false rocks. The dark hump they saw was Louie the Great Trained Walrus, direct from the Bering Straits, the Smartest Walrus in Captivity. To further the illusion, Kaybach dumped a wheelbarrow load of ice cubes into the fetid water. He explained that Louie communicated with standard head shakes, and could clap his flippers in mathematical tally.

He called my name and I plunged off the rocks and through the shallow water. By squatting inside the oilskin bag, I could make Louie appear to rear on his haunches.

"Are you a girl walrus?"

I vigorously shook my head no.

"He's a male, folks! Take a look at those tusks. We lost three Eskimos capturing him. Very sad." A pause for the audience to consider their own danger. "Are you married, Louie?"

Again I shook my head.

"You got a girlfriend, Louie?"

I shook my head.

"Do you want one?"

This was my cue to launch myself across the pool toward the nearest woman in the audience. She usually screamed and people backed away. Kaybach yelled at me to settle down. I appeared to defy him momentarily before slinking back to the center of the pool. By this time, enough water had leaked in to make my skin slimy.

"You know how bachelors are, folks," Kaybach continued with a broad wink. "And everyone knows what seafood does to a fellow."

He asked a few more questions—what state we were in, who the local mayor was—arranging a multiple choice for me to answer yes or no. When I was correct, he threw a dead fish which I forced through the mouth flap to lie cold and smelly against my chest. Kaybach told the audience that I could only count to ten and invited them to stump me with problems of arithmetic. Someone asked the sum of five plus two. Kaybach yelled the question to me and I clapped my front flippers seven times. After a few more tests, a circus plant bullied his way to the front and shouted that he'd seen this on TV and it was a fake. He said the walrus was trained to respond only to the voice of its master, who spoke in code. Kaybach assured everyone that this was not true. He suggested that the man ask his own question, providing the answer didn't go past ten.

"Square roots," the plant said.

"What's that?" Kaybach asked.

"A number times itself." The plant turned to the crowd. "You know, from high school. The square root of a hundred is ten because ten times ten is a hundred."

The audience nodded and the plant faced me. "Okay, Louie, what's the square root of nine?"

He turned his back again and showed three fingers so that the audience could see, but not me. Kaybach began to stutter a protest. The plant shut him up and asked me again. To build suspense, I waited thirty seconds before clapping my flippers three times.

The audience always applauded, as much to see a bully get shut down by a walrus as for the answer. The plant shook his head in disbelief. Kaybach tossed a fish and asked the final question.

"Are you a walrus, Louie?"

I shook my head no.

"Oh, I guess you think you're human, then."

I nodded very fast.

"I'm sorry, Louie. You're nothing but a walrus. You'll never be a man."

I sank into the water, performed an awkward circling manuever, and scuttled behind a rock. Kaybach thanked everyone and asked for a big hand for a walrus so smart that he knew genuine sadness— he'd never be a human.

I had a half-hour break before beginning again with a new plant and a different fake question. I had become a circus performer, or in Barney's parlance, a kinker. The name came from the effects of the nightlong wagon rides in the old days, after which the performers spent a couple of hours stretching kinks from their bodies.

The various sideshows were tucked into a midway of carny games as crooked as a dog's hind leg. Even the benign ring toss and dart throw were rigged. The con operators allowed a few people to win large, highly visible prizes. They picked the winners carefully. The best investments were young couples, or a family that moved as a group. Forced to carry the prize the rest of their visit, the winners served as advertising. Many people won at the start of the day; none toward the end.

As a full-fledged kinker, I had access to the forbidden zone of performer alley. Here the clowns played chess, the aerialists disdained anyone confined to earth, and the dwarfs spent most of their time baiting the Parrot Lady. They constantly threatened to pluck her, and commented quite openly on her presumed skill at fellatio.

One Sunday, in a community so religious the circus wasn't allowed to admit the public until well past noon, the heat rose to ninety-eight. Only the aerialists and the Parrot Lady had trailers with air-conditioning. The rest of us sat semiclothed in available shade. The dwarfs began crooning a love song on the Parrot Lady's aluminum steps. She opened her door with enough force to smack it against the trailer. The dwarfs retreated like tumbleweed.

"A bird in hand," one said.

"Is worth a hand in the bush," said the other.

"I got a sword she can't swallow."

"Get lost, you little pissants," the Parrot Lady said. She leaned against the doorjamb in the shimmering heat. "Hey, Walrus Man," she called. "Come here."

All the kinkers blinked from a doze, staring at me, then at her. I stumbled to her trailer as if moving through fog. My clothes clung to me.

"Save me a sandwich," said one of the dwarfs.

The air-conditioned trailer made the sweat cold on my body. She motioned me to a couch. Gingham curtains hung from each window, and an autographed picture of Elvis Presley sat on a tiny TV. The room was very small, very neat.

"Thirsty?" she said. "Like a drink?"

I nodded and she poured clear liquid from a pitcher into a glass, added ice and an olive.

"Nothing better in summer than a martini," she said.

Not wanting her to know that I'd never sampled such an exotic drink, I drank it in one chug and asked for another. She lifted her eyebrows and poured me one. I drank half for the sake of civility.

"The one thing I hate more than dwarfs," she said, "is the circus."

She wore a long white dress with a high collar and sleeves that ran to her wrists. No tattoos were visible. A rowing machine occupied a third of the trailer's space. She topped my drink and filled her own glass.

"This is my fourth circus," she said. "I've worked with fat ladies, bearded women, Siamese twins, rubber-skinned people, and midgets. The three-legged man. A giant. Freaks by nature, all freaks but me."

"Not you."

She offered her glass for a toast and I drained mine. She filled it again. We sat across from each other. The room was so narrow our knees touched.

"They hate me because they can't understand why someone would choose to be a freak. It took me five years to get tattooed. You can't do it all at once. I had the best artists in the country tattoo me."

"Did it hurt?"

"That's the main part of it. Freaks have to hurt and I wanted mine real. Everyone can see that I'm a freak now. I finally suffered for real to get there."

I nodded, confused. A row of dolls stood on a shelf bracketed to the wall. She poured more drinks and settled into the chair. Her ankles were primly crossed, exposing only her toes. She wore no jewelry.

"I hate them because they're what I was in secret, before the tattoos. I was a freak too. You just couldn't tell. I was tired of hurting on the inside, like them. I hate my tattoos and I hate the men who pay to see them. Nobody knows about my inside. The rest of the freaks are the opposite. They're normal inside but stuck in a freak's body. Not me."

"I don't know what you're talking about."

"That's why I'm telling you."

"What?"

"I can't have children."

I sipped my drink. I wanted a cigarette but didn't see an ashtray. I didn't know what to say.

"Yes," I said.

"That's the sweetest thing anyone's ever said to me."

"You could adopt."

"Shut up!" she said. "I've seen ads in the paper for adoption. 'Call collect,' they say. 'All expenses paid.' I won't buy a baby. You better go. Don't tell anyone anything. Let them believe we fucked like minks."

I stood and fell sideways on the couch. Moving slowly, I got to the door and turned to say goodbye. Her pale hands covered her face. She was crying.

"I love those dwarfs," she said. "They're my kids."

I opened the door and made it to the bottom step before falling. The difference in temperature was swift and hard as a roundhouse blow. Someone helped me stand. The dust on my skin turned to mud from my abrupt sweating. An aerialist walked me to a truck and lay me in the shade.

An hour later Kaybach kicked me awake, berating me for being late, though he'd heard the reason. I staggered after him. Con men and kinkers wiggled their eyebrows, winked and grinned. A female equestrian caressed me with her gaze as if I were the last wild mustang out of the Bighorns. I barely had time to wriggle into my costume before Kaybach began herding the suckers in.

Our tent had no ventilation and was ten degrees hotter than outside. The water in the pool had a skin on the surface. When I lay down on the fake rocks, the world began spinning. Closing my eyes made me twice as dizzy. From a great distance Kaybach called his cue and I realized that he had been yelling for some time. I slid into the nasty water.

I managed to get through the preliminary routines with Kaybach's patient repetition of cue. He threw a fish as reward, which I dutifully tucked inside the mouth flap. Its body was swollen from heat. Mixed with fish stink was the heavy odor of gin oozing from my pores. I clenched my teeth to quell nausea. While Kaybach spieled about my intelligence, I shoved the dead fish back into the water. The smell clung to my chin and face. Water had seeped through the eye slits, encasing me in an amnion of scum. My head throbbed. As long as I didn't move, my belly remained under control.

Kaybach asked the yes-or-no questions. I squatted to make the walrus rear on his haunches, each movement an effort. The mask felt welded to my head. Kaybach threw a fish that bounced off my torso. The thought of retrieving it ruined me. My belly folded in on itself, and I knew that the spew would suffocate me. Kaybach was yelling. My face poured sweat.

I pulled my hands from the flipper compartments, worked my arms into position, and treated the crowd to the rare sight of a walrus decapitating itself. The mask splashed into the water. I retched a stream that arced from Louie's neck. Kaybach stepped into the pool and yelled for everyone to leave. People were screaming and demanding refunds.

I swam to the safety of my fake ice floe. Water had gushed into the oilskin suit, and briefly I feared drowning. I left the costume in the water, crawled to the edge of the tent, lifted the canvas and inhaled. The hundred-degree air tasted sweet and glorious. Sideshow tents were butted against the big top with a small space in between for stakes and ropes. I fled down the alley in my underwear. Peaches and Barney were gone from the truck. I rinsed my body in a tub of her drinking water and dressed in my extra clothes. The parking lot was a rolling field with beat-down grass. Locals worked it for a few bucks and a free pass. The third car picked me up. Twenty minutes later I stood in a town, the name of which I didn't know.

I oriented myself so the setting sun lay on my left, and began walking north. The Drinking Gourd emerged at dusk. Kentucky produced both Abe Lincoln and Jeff Davis. Like Kentuckians of the Civil War, I was loyal to no direction. I was neither kinker nor freak, yankee nor reb, boss nor bum. I wasn't much of a playwright either.

Autumn has fled in a blur of wind and leaves. The first frost never let up, clamping cold to the earth. Rita is now nine months and one week pregnant. If the baby doesn't volunteer soon, the doctor will induce its birth in a week. Beside the front door is a suitcase packed with food, diapers, cigars, a deck of cards, and a baby-naming book that reminds me of a wildlife identification guide. Rita is weary of her awkward gait, my incessant presence underfoot. I am powerless to comfort her. She listens to an inner music and I hear only the tow of the woods.

The sky is domed solid blue, pale at the edges as if the world floats inside a balloon. Beyond the perimeter lies endless time, an absence of gravity and light, the very world in which our child exists. The fetus is said to dream in utero. I suppose it must recall the passage of its own brief time—the fifth week of its gills and tail, the later limbless period when its organs were blooming. At week twenty-six it forms bones. A month later the brain doubles, increasing its capacity to dream.

Last night I dreamed that Rita gave birth to a boy who was also my father. I became the middle man, discarded and ignored. This morning Rita lay on her side with hands clasped below her bulging belly, as if proffering her child to the world. She said the baby kicked all night. I stoked the fire and left for the woods.

Wind pushes snow away from the river, forming a powder that shifts like vapor. These ground blizzards demolish vision. It is as if one walks through a haze of chalk. Because I would prefer a son, I say that I want a girl so as not to be disappointed. Rita is honest. She stakes her claim for a boy-child early, choosing faith in her own biology. She has no use for common hope.

There are more females born per year because the X sperm lives slightly longer while hunting the egg. Less likely to be born, men are more prone to death. I am the first son of a first son of a first son, and I want to continue the cycle. Rita says it is a boy. I hope she knows.

Cold air numbs my face above my beard. On certain days the radio forbids pregnant women from drinking tap water. We buy it in gallon jugs, wondering when the amnion will break. Rita recently woke from a nap lying in dampness, the sheets cold against her flesh. She called to me, her voice excited, certain that the time had come. I raced to her side. The sheets were stained pale violet, a color that scared me. My mouth was dry. I rubbed the sheet and sniffed my fingers, surprised at the faint scent of grapes. Rita rolled over. Buried in the blankets beside her was an empty glass of juice. Laughter arrived, always overdue, evidence of life.

Last month offered a blue moon, the second full moon in the same month. It was the brightest moon of our lifetime, closer to earth than any time since 1912. Both coasts were drenched by enormous tides. Since humans are sixty percent water, perpetually hauling eleven gallons inside our bodies, the moon affects us, too. I thought it might draw the baby from the womb, but Rita didn't even have Braxton-Hicks, contractions that are known as false labor pains. First-time mothers take longer to give the baby up. First-time fathers, I've found, take longer to get to sleep at night.

Rita is the focus of our lives, her belly the pinpoint. I feel the futility of a laid-off worker, the fading sense of being useful. I am left with the memory of our last sex two months ago, in which the child had literally come between us, or swayed below. I'd felt as though I were trespassing, hoping not to damage whatever lived inside.

The wind halts abruptly and I see faint fox tracks at the bottom of a rise. Blown snow fills the upwind side of the prints, which remind me more of a cat than a dog. I follow the trail, aware that seeing a wild animal requires giving up hope, the same way Rita has abandoned her hope for gender. She simply knows. Wind whips mist in the air and I crouch, aiming my face along the path of tracks. Snow is against my eyes, down my collar. My bad knee begins to ache. The fox never hunts with hope for prey, but with *yarak*, an Arabic word without English equivalent that means "hunting condition, ready to kill." As we lost our animal instincts, we replaced them with the veils of reason, love, superstition, and hope. No fox ever hoped for gender. Only humanity hopes, which makes us the most hopeless.

At birth my child's brain will be equal in size to the brain of a baby gorilla. My father is bald and toothless, exactly the way he was born. By prolonging childhood, we are able to learn the alphabet, mathematics, the sense of awe and doubt, how to kill for pleasure. The palm of a Down's baby has two lines instead of three, like that of an ape. My father's palm is often damp. When I made mistakes as a child, he referred to me as a cretin, and I felt proud, believing it meant I was from the island of Crete. I hope for a son who is not like me.

Cardinals slice the air like drops of blood. The wind slows, leaving a drift against a sapling, a larger drift on the parent tree. The fox prints have faded into the swept forest floor and I move in the direction they were headed, trying to imagine the fox making detours around piles of brush, angling for the water's edge. Ice floes drift in silence. A daughter makes better sense because I'm liable to do more damage to a son. It is my heritage, my instinct, as powerful as a barred owl's claws in the back of a squirrel.

The trunks of maples along the river are too large for their height, the roots having sucked water for decades, expanding their bodies but not their boughs. They have overevolved, like the Spartan, the Roman, the ancient dwellers of Crete. Wind from the south coats the side of each maple with snow. The other side grows moss. Various animals live in their hollow bodies, kicking all night. A child grows within Rita's belly and I hope that my professed hope for a girl goes unanswered. Ahead of me the fox knows better than to hope I leave. It merely waits, knowing that I will go.

I follow the river through the morning air of snow like smoke. My sister was the first female Little Leaguer in our county; my aunt, Kentucky's first female CPA; my grandmother, the first in the family to graduate from high school. The women in my family fare better than the men. They live longer, destroy less, know better than to hope. I still want a son, the dream of many men.

Near the treeline I find fresh fox prints and realize it has doubled back on me, and since I am here now, it has probably doubled back again. The fox is watching me watch my thoughts. None of it matters—not gender, hope, or even health. It's all over anyhow, decided nine months back, moments after the final cellular brawl of fertilization. The embryo is sexless until the fourth month, when genitals begin to grow. Roman women who failed to produce a male heir were put to death, but we now understand that the flailing sperm decides the gender. A son will carry the family name; a daughter carries the child.

Rabbit tracks lead to a patch of scattered leaves the color of pennies found in gravel. The immense hind legs of a rabbit prevents it from walking backwards. A woodcock can see three hundred sixty degrees without turning its head, but we are the only species capable of hindsight. Rita says she cannot remember when she wasn't pregnant. She no longer recalls her sleeping dreams.

An itinerant coyote treed a coon yesterday, then continued roaming downriver, rare for Iowa. Wind has cleared the tracks away. I envy its reckless lifestyle—the solitary animal seeking fun like the romanticized single man, perpetual bachelor, the lone-wolf cowboy of books and film. The beauty of the coyote is its inability to ponder the past. It is happy in a pack or on its own, honoring the moon, the cycle of women. Very soon my freedom will end. No one is perfect but fathers are expected to be.

I wedge into a tight gap amid three maples that splay the sky. Seedpods lie between my feet. The sun won't melt the snow till spring. In the fifth century, Pindar wrote that man is but a dream of a shadow. Rita has long dreamed of a child. My father dreams of an heir. In the shadow world of Rita's womb, the fetus dreams of more space. I think of the future, of my adult child smuggling me from the hospital to die in the woods. Trees dream about the death of an ax. The snowflake dreams of finding its twin.

Walking home is work, trudging into the wind. My feet are slowed by old snow beneath the scuttling powder of today. My mind is the circling fox, sure of instinct, heading for its den. In the house I tell Rita of my thoughts, that nothing matters. She disagrees. "Everything matters now," she says. "More than ever."

A week passed thumbing north, my sextant aimed at New England, as determined as Columbus. I stormed the region, convinced of discovering a higher level of civilization absent from the rest of the country. Instead, I found a room in Salem, Massachusetts, with a renegade Pole named Shadrack. Every door in our apartment had been robbed of its knob. Nothing locked. Our single common room was a large windowless kitchen full of dirty dishes. Stray trash surrounded the garbage can like drifted snow.

The first night we met, Shadrack confided that a single yoni hair was stronger than a team of oxen. His life was shimmed at all the joints and he'd taken to shimming the shims. During winter, he slept in a lime-green tent pitched in the kitchen. In exchange for acting as a security guard, Shadrack had a painting studio in an abandoned chalk factory by the river. Chalk dust covered him like a corpse risen from the lime. He was the perfect friend for me—so starved for company that he talked to mice in his studio.

I had quit painting to write, and he was a poet who now painted. We were inverted Siamese twins, connected at the intellect. He'd never completed a painting, which gave him an edge over me since I had yet to begin a play. When the time came, I'd write a single script that would not only eliminate the need for more but nullify the prevailing theater. One play would mortar my manhood into a wall.

My adherence to the journal slid into a strange realm where I viewed my immediate interactions as a form of living diary. If riding a bicycle through a snowstorm sounded like good material for the journal, I borrowed a bike in a blizzard. The actual ride didn't matter. What I did was try to observe myself as carefully as possible, while simultaneously imagining myself writing everything down later

Shadrack's current project consisted of sculpture assembled with objects he stole from his friends. When something turned up missing, I merely had to visit his studio and surreptitiously steal it back. If he caught me, he'd complain that I was violating the sanctity of his work. A prolonged argument ensued until I offered to trade him another piece of my property. His attitude toward money was slightly more evolved, in that he never stole it. If I had cash, Shadrack demanded some. I hesitated before realizing that not only would he eventually pay it back but the practice granted me license to take his money as well. We once lived for two months on the same ten bucks passed to and fro. Knowing he either owed me money or would lend me some took the edge off hunger and despair..

The circus had given me a taste for working outdoors, and I quickly ran through three jobs—at a car wash, as a landscaper, and selling flowers from a pushcart. I got to know Salem, founded in 1626, now decayed and gift-wrapped like a mummy's womb. After the failure of its harbor and mills, the town relied on its shameful history for tourist money. The high school ball teams were called the Witches. A church had recently been converted to a witch museum. Visitors poked their heads through loose-fitting stocks for a photograph to show the relatives.

Salem's original settlers were so molded by Calvinism that they regarded the natives as either devils or the lost tribe of Israel. I seemed to fall into the first category. As in New York, my accent betrayed me, I had no local references, and my job résumé didn't impress anyone. I applied for jobs at which I was grossly unqualified, simply to create theater for my subsequent journal entry. When the cash flow between Shadrack and me became lopsided, I concocted a false history and tried for my first professional job. I bought a white shirt from a thrift shop and used black spray paint to make a pair of brown shoes acceptable for an interview. A bar/restaurant hired me as a waiter.

Between art projects Shadrack chased women and read science books, considering himself a lay physicist. My ineptitude with women perplexed him, a phenomenon he viewed with the same curiosity he had for quantum mechanics. As an experiment, he introduced me to private school women who spoke with immobile lips, already worried about lining their future faces with too much expression. Their habitual lockjaw reminded me of a boy back home who'd been bitten by a rabid dog. The kid's father killed the dog, cut off its head, and mailed it to Frankfort for analysis of the brain. Over the course of a season, the boy received a hundred injections in the belly as cure. I often wondered what the scientists would find in a sample dipped from the windblown cortex of those coastal women.

Shadrack called them trout and regarded their seduction as sport. He appointed himself my fishing tutor, steering me through faceless singles bars murky with cocaine. He deeply envied the blue whale, possessor of a nine-foot lingam it can harden at will. Though I was a lousy pupil, Shadrack never tired of lecturing me. Fishing was easy physics, according to him.

"You must maximize your options with a matrix of lines," he said. "Trust the bait and forget about subject matter. Remember Newton's laws of motion. You must behave as a particle wave. Stay away from sandbars, red giants, and octopi. Don't be afraid to let the trout wander. And remember, Chris, never ever yank your rod."

Five nights a week we trawled the many neighborhood streams, hauling our lines at closing time. Mine were always empty. My efforts at picking up women were absurd at best—I could never get past the notion of what I was up to, and assumed that the women knew too. The whole courtship dance seemed archaic, silly, and expensive.

To honor Shadrack in the Eastern sense, I went ahead one night with the subatomic anonymous sex. The woman and I were both quite drunk. We walked to her place. She pressed me deep into an easy chair, where my zipper parted like the jaws of life. She climbed

aboard and impaled herself, pinning me odd-angled against the
chair. Her face strained toward the ceiling, eyes shut, neck veins
pulsing. Flush against me, her hips began vibrating like lunch trays
in a tremor. Her sweat and spit dripped to my shirt. The chair
rapped the windowpane in a frenzied rhythm. Everything hurt and
I felt dizzy. Her body finally sagged, quaking and shuddering in a
gradual meltdown. Our interface had ended with us more clothed
than nude.

She peeled herself away, leaving my lingam hard as basalt, throbbing for release. She moved to the bed. I thought perhaps we were
shifting to a more comfortable position, but when I lay beside her,
she was crying. I was completely befuddled.

"Don't look at me," she said.

"It's dark anyhow."

"This isn't right."

"I know."

"You know?" she said.

"It's not easy to sleep with someone you don't know."

"It used to be."

"That's a good sign."

"You're not mad?" she asked.

"Why should I be mad?"

"The guy last week was mad."

"I should go."

She gently pulled me beside her. She wore a small golden ear of
corn around her neck, a *shibboleth*. I moved to reap in silence. As
Shadrack would say, our shared electrons produced a brief covalent
bond and I snuck away early. Waking up hung over and inter-
twined with a stranger was worse than the hoosegow.

A few days later I mentioned the sordid mess to Shadrack, who
suggested I upgrade my haunts. He'd begun ransacking tourist bars
for a wealthy woman to raise a flock of blue-eyed athletic kids. His
future wife's earlobes must be attached to her head. He dated heir-
esses to old money and new money, the daughters of politicians and

industrialists. He never quite learned that many women enjoy brief flings with artistic men. Legs opened like scissors at the chance to aggravate Daddy by introducing a scoundrel to the gene pool. No family wanted one of us in the woodpile, especially fresh-cut hardwood like myself.

Shadrack escorted me to a fancy tavern with a three-piece combo playing jazz in a corner. The musicians and waiters were wearing suits. Shadrack had lent me a tie, but I felt like a fugitive whose story everyone knew. He ordered a mixed drink of a strange hue and smell, saying it helped cover his halitosis, a product of his decaying teeth which chipped away like pearls. He was watching a woman with a perfectly nostriled nose. I suggested he introduce himself.

"I don't know," he said. "Every time I look at her, I think of my old girlfriend. That makes me remember the one before her and then I think of my mother. When I think of my mother, I think of the Virgin Mary and then I remember how Joseph never got laid. So maybe I'll talk to her for Joseph's sake."

He strode away, a man no taller than a broomstick, with the sterling posture of a career officer. His natural walk crested with a toe bounce that gained him an extra inch of height. I scanned the gleaming row of bottles behind the bar and ordered a shot of triple sec. The bartender gave me a peculiar look which pleased me; only the truly privileged drank it straight. I ordered another and another.

A few hours passed before I lurched from the bar and began walking home. I woke lying on my back in a softness that reminded me of grass. Sea gulls gave their mournful call. My head hurt. I closed my eyes against what was certainly a dream, and later woke in the same place. Slowly I realized that the lovely blue was genuine sky and I was outside. My clothes were damp with dew. I turned my head and the grass continued to expand across a vast amount of treeless space. A panicked awareness burrowed into me that I had passed out on a rich man's lawn. I rolled to my knees and swallowed to prevent gagging. My belly felt straight-wired to my brain.

A low dirt mound rose in the distance. I was in Salem High's outfield. I crawled toward the foul line and slept in the shade of a padlocked hot dog stand. I never drank triple sec again.

A few weeks later the mail brought a letter from my brother advising me in no uncertain terms that I was to be best man at his wedding. Twenty-nine years ago, my parents had moved very deep into the hills to drop a litter in private. They discouraged both family branches from visiting, violating the premise of Appalachian culture. Mom and Dad explained that it was for our own sake. I had no history behind my father, no love beyond my mother. As adults, none of us wrote or called. What had begun as a tight-knit cloister now functioned as a barricade. We had become the very people our parents sought to protect us from—distant family members.

I called Dane collect and said I'd thumb down, hoping he would withdraw his request. Instead, he offered to fetch me and I reluctantly agreed, terrified at having him bear witness to my circumstances. The terror turned to rage at my brother for getting married before me. As oldest, it was my right. The anger gave way to a bleak depression as I realized I'd never been to a wedding and didn't know any married people. Getting married was something full-fledged adults did; I was still struggling through a prolonged adolescence, Columbus lost in the fog. As an only child, though, my namesake had been spared the perils of a brother. Dane probably felt the same way.

Dane and I were very close until my behavior veered to the illegal. Our break came when I stole an electric football game to clean the seeds from a quarter-pound of marijuana. The gentle vibration worked perfectly but Dane didn't share my pride at ingenuity. He was outraged by the tiny seeds rolling into the end zone.

A few months later the county sheriff banged at the door with a warrant for Dane's arrest. Mom cried and Dad's face paled beneath the strain of incredulity. I watched from the bathroom, fully aware that the wrong name was on the warrant. I marched to the door and gave myself up in what remains my most heroic act to date. Dad was less angry at me than at the foolhardy notion of going to court at seven A.M.

Several years later, the night before I left Kentucky, Dane and I lay talking in our flanking beds. He said that he worried about me, and I asked why.

"You don't have goals, Chris. You just want to go. You don't check your progress and you can't see where you're heading. If you can't prove the answer, it's all messed up. Know what I mean?"

While I contemplated the truth of his words, he began to snore. Dane was a mathematician whose life moved along an advanced formula of direct lines, bracketed exponents, congruent functions, and the ultimate goal of symmetry. He had no room for my random patterns of oblique and gleeful entropy. Dane could prove the world was round without ever leaving his room. I needed wind, a flagship, and open water.

When I asked for time off work to attend the wedding, the manager of the restaurant said not to come back. I greeted Dane with the news that I'd been fired for his wedding, trapping him into complicity with my lifestyle. He couldn't scold me, as he had in the past. I felt full of myself, like a hand puppet turned inside out.

Shadrack had recently learned the word "hodad" from a crossword puzzle, and we organized a hodad party. He and a friend with a green mohawk painted a beach mural on a wall.

"Are them boys all right?" Dane asked.

"Yup. They're artists."

"Ain't queer, are they?"

"No. They're friends of mine. It'll be a great party, Dane."

"What the heck's a hodad?"

"A guy who hangs around the beach, pretending to be a surfer."

"Like you and art."

I turned up the stereo. Angry voices bellowed off key. Dane plugged in a bluegrass tape and somebody stomped it after ten seconds. Promising to replace it, I introduced Dane to a woman with a pierced nose. Our only window shattered into the street, venting the acrid haze of cannabis. At midnight a second wave of people arrived with another blast of hysteric energy. Cocaine flowed like twin white train rails.

Periodically I checked on my dismayed brother, who wandered my dump with his feed store cap bobbing above the exuberant crowd. He became grimmer and grimmer. The party peaked at three A.M. and people slowly trickled away, the floor squeaking underfoot from spilt beer. Shadrack was busy with the pierced-nose woman beneath the kitchen table.

I offered Dane my bed. He shook his head, holding the smashed bluegrass tape in his big hands. An empty coke vial crunched below his boot. I waited for him to speak so I could condemn his choice. He knew better, as always. The expression on his face reminded me of our father's contempt, and I got mad.

"You're too young to get married," I said.

"Maybe," he said. "But you're too old to live like this."

I went to my room and closed the door. In the morning we began an argument that lasted the next several years. By the time we reached Kentucky, Dane and I had not spoken for over five hundred miles. He reluctantly agreed that I was right—I should have hitchhiked. After Columbus's third trip across the sea, he was brought home in manacles and chains. I knew how he felt.

We turned onto the dirt road up our hill, and drove along the ridge to our house. Vines on the south wall clung thick as snakes. My sisters, Jeanie and Sue, rushed across the yard, gave us each a kiss, and entered the house with Dane. Mom stepped from the porch and hugged me, rocking like a jonquil in the wind. She escorted me into the kitchen, where Dad stood beside the stove. Mom stayed in the middle, a demilitarized zone.

Dad and I regarded each other like a brace of roosters. I stiffened my shoulders. Seeing a familiar reaction, he relaxed and offered a beer, the family grease for social interaction. We settled into our former bunkers at opposite corners of the kitchen, separated by the stove. After several years, we had returned to the site of countless vicious conflicts which I'd always lost. During the Civil War, Kentucky was notorious for pitting son against father, brother against brother.

Dad and I gulped our beer through a strange new gauze of respect. I'd stayed away, had never asked for money. His hair was white and he had a belly. He was losing his family to the outside world and there was no replacement. We drank another beer, discussing safe topics that neither of us cared about. He slowly realized that I would not rise to his bait, while I saw him as he was—a man unsure of how to face an adult son. He was stiffly cordial, treating me like an ambassador from an enemy country that had recently signed a treaty. This hill, I realized, belonged irrevocably to Dad. He was Ferdinand ruling Portugal, and he could keep it. I had the New World.

An hour later Mom marshaled the family to the table. Everyone sat in their accustomed seats. For years supper had been nightly and common, with tardiness promptly punished. Now we were disbanding like a riverboat crew confronted by the railroad's swift competition.

I offered to hold the rings for Dane and he refused.

"Why not?" I said. "Afraid I might pawn them for tux money?"

"Don't you have it?" he said.

"They're gray, with a swallowtail," Jeanie said. "We're picking them up tomorrow in Lexington. Forty dollars is cheap for a tuxedo."

"Not cheap enough," I muttered.

"Some were a hundred dollars," Sue said. "They were black velvet. But gray goes with pink and that's what us girls are wearing."

"You got it or not?" Dane glared at me.

I glanced quickly around the table. Mom stared at her plate. My sisters were smiling at how nice we'd look. Dad chewed the ham bone, its end small and round as a snake's eye.

"No, Dane," I said. "I don't."

"You could have broke down and got a job."

"For a tux?"

"For me!" He pushed from the table. "You should see how he lives! Not a pot to piss in or a window to throw it out of. And he wants to hold my damn rings. One of his girlfriends had a ring in her nose like a root hog."

"Is that true?" asked Jeanie.

"Yup," I said. "On the side, though. Not in the middle."

"Good thing she doesn't have hay fever," Dad said.

Jeanie and Sue giggled, while Mom smiled. Dane gripped the chairback so hard the veins on his hands quivered.

"It's not funny," he said. "No wonder he doesn't bring girls home. They do it under the table up there."

"That wasn't me, Dane."

"Your yankee buddy done it."

"Shad's like a brother to me."

"What's wrong with the one you got?"

"If I weren't your best man, I'd tell you."

Dad slammed the ham bone against the table like a gun barrel. The sound echoed in the small room.

"That'll do, boys."

Dane left the room, his big feet stomping the pine slat floor. Now that Dad and I enjoyed a cease-fire, I'd attacked my brother. For all my wayward ways, I was still the favored son and Dane was relegated to piloting the *Niña*, running aground on his own efforts to please the family.

Mom spoke, gentle as rain. "The evening before we got married, your daddy ran his truck through a pasture gate."

"I'm not a gate."

"He's not much of a truck," Dad said. "Let him be. Lord knows we've all let you be."

The next day everyone but me drove to Lexington for the tuxedos. I went down the hill to my old stone grade school. Every

Halloween I'd carried stolen feed corn onto the roof and hauled Dane up by his belt. I would give him half my corn and we'd shower passing cars with the kernels, rattling them like Demeter's sleet. Other boys from the hill screamed at their brothers like dogs; Dane and I had waited until we were adults to fight. In three months he was going to graduate school on a computer scholarship. Though I'd left first, he no longer needed me. I resented the loss.

I walked home well past dark and ate leftovers alone. The family seemed scared of me, a change from my childhood role. My job then had been to head off trouble by saying something funny, diverting attention. Now I'd become the trouble. I lay on the couch, drank a pint, and went to sleep.

We drove to the church early and changed clothes in a back room. The tux fit a little too tight. My grandmother and Aunt Lou arrived in a flourish of dacron. Cousins appeared, distant uncles and aunts, a hermitic great-uncle with his third wife. My old buddy J.J. roared his pirate hot rod into the lot, windows streaming rock music and marijuana smoke.

The family of the bride was polite and charming, although their Southern Baptist beliefs opposed them to coffee, cigarettes, alcohol, dancing, and me. Ellen's clan outnumbered us three to one, but we had them buffaloed. The only other male in the wedding party was Dane's college roommate from Saudi Arabia. Seeing Ahmed, Ellen's family gasped, fearing that he might just be a black man. Ahmed hung on my arm like a virgin in a strip bar, his accent thick in my ear.

"Chrees. I never been to a Chreestian church before."

"Hey, everybody," I bellowed. "This here's Ahmed! He's from the Middle East!"

Group tension flitted away like a lynch rope tucked from sight. I left him with J.J. and searched the church for Dane, who was vomiting in the men's room behind a locked stall. I climbed onto the pristine sink and leaned over the partition.

"You'll be all right," I said.

Dane gagged and retched. The stench rose, palpable as river sludge. My foot slid off the sink and I tumbled to the tile, landing spread-eagle on my back. Dane staggered from the stall.

"You split your pants, Chris."

"And you've got puke on your ascot."

He helped me up and we swapped ties. If I walked carefully, the swallowtail would conceal the ripped seam. Dane gave me the rings. Each of us waited for the other to initiate a hug, but the mutual need made us incapable and afraid. Knowing we wanted to was almost enough. We shook hands across the urinal.

The families bunched the chapel like cheering sections at a homecoming game. The king and queen grandly strode the center aisle, followed by Jeanie and Ahmed, then Sue and me. Every few steps I lit candles with a four-foot flame rod that responded to a trigger in its handle.

The air filled with candle smoke, weeping, and the photographer's flash. Half blinded by the strobe, Ahmed stumbled into Jeanie, who dropped her bouquet. I bent to pick it up and the flame rod swung wild, clipping Ellen's great-aunt across the temple. Our procession continued until we faced the holy man, a chubby guy with a pitted nose. After the mumbo jumbo, he stared at the puke on my ascot and asked for the rings. My clan gained a sister and a daughter. Her family lost on all fronts.

The reception room was hot and we carried our watery punch to the parking lot. I hunted the great-aunt to apologize. She was still in the church bragging that the Lord had touched her during the ceremony. Her companion winked and waved me away. Outside, pockets of family squared off like gangs in a street fight. Our linked tribes milled about, smiling without touching, obeying invisible picket lines. We were a black sheep flock mired by secrets that everyone knew. Feud and subterfuge etched our past.

"I'm in the restaurant business," I told everyone. "Be opening my own place soon. Business is for me."

I tarried in the lot, watching blood-kin strangers depart as furtively as they had come. My tux itched. After quick goodbyes, J.J. and I vaulted into his car and roared away. The family had come together like a handful of uneven strands temporarily spliced. We were Penelope's filament, secretly unraveled each night, then rewoven for public sight.

J.J. popped open the glove box and tossed a bottle of amphetamines in my lap. Melancholy melted into time-released segments of joy. He dropped me off in Indiana and I hitchhiked north.

Beneath a tree outside of Scranton, Pennsylvania, I snuggled into my sleeping bag. The Milky Way spread across the chilly sky and I gave up on being a playwright. It was not free enough, was dependent on director, actor, set designer, even the audience. I decided to become a poet. My life was already flowing along lines that, if not poetic, were too grim to consider. As in hitchhiking, there were no rules in poetry. What few poems I'd read had dispensed with punctuation, logic, and rhyme—all severe restrictions to my dormant creativity. Poems were often short, which would allow me to flourish in the realm.

I zipped the bag tight and pulled into a ball. I felt as if I might explode and implode simultaneously. When I stopped fighting, the tears arrived. The scent of exhaust drifted from the highway. The ground was soft, a comfort.

Dane did everything properly, made all the correct decisions. He had a lovely wife, would eventually own nice things, and make the standard visits home. None of it mattered. He could never overcome the betrayal of a family that had always loved me more than him. My wild behavior was a prolonged effort to get out from under the burden, and I wondered if the opposite was true for Dane. If so, I hoped he didn't realize it. One poet per family was enough.

My return to Salem possessed all the heralded pomp of a rising ghost. I was determined to live, breathe, and eat poetry. In a fit of creativity, I taped photographs of great poets to the edge of a mirror and hung it above my desk. As long as I sat facing the mirror, my face joined their ranks, and I belonged with them. I spent most of my time peeking at the mirror from across the room, waiting for inspiration. Twice I sat at the desk. An incredible tension rose within me. My stomach hurt, and I could not grasp a pencil. There was poetry in the mirror but I had no idea how to get it out. The photographs mocked me. My mind felt like an old brick.

I scrounged a night job washing dishes at a bar near the water-front. Free beer and food propped the low pay. The weather turned cold and I spent my days at the library for warmth, joining the rest of Salem's kooks. We all claimed chairs in the periodical room, pretending to read beneath the librarian's hostile gaze. When one of our band died, everyone moved up a seat, closer to the radiator. Rather than reading poems, I scribbled essays about the sheer joy of poetry, proclaiming poets as the true masters of language. Being one was vastly more important than committing verse to paper. The more pages I filled in my diary, the more I felt like a genuine bard.

Shadrack moved to Boston, and I could no longer afford to rent our dump. I crashed with a sympathetic waitress, who let me sleep in a hammock suspended in her kitchen. Eventually we began making sorties into each other's rooms. At the end of a year she left me for a Navy Seal because, as she said, "He knows what he wants from life." I explained that poetry was just as valid as fastening bombs to enemy ships. She shot from the hip, barely aiming, and nailed me in my own cross hairs—I hadn't written a poem since we'd met.

When she asked for help moving, I agreed, thinking she would change her mind. After two days of divisive labor, she gave me a warm six-pack and took the hammock away. I slept on the floor. Boone had said that no Indian who claimed to be a friend had ever deceived him but you could never trust New Englanders.

The Iowa sky is a gray mosaic seen through bare tree limbs. Rita is uncomfortable in every position. Our child performs acrobatics within the placental tautness of her belly. Her urination has taken on the obsessive quality of a hobby and is the source of all conversation. At night the temperature drops to twenty below. Windchill reduces the air to negative sixty, offering the chance of death within five minutes. Skin will freeze in seconds.

While sleeping, Rita cradles her belly with her forearms, backside shoving against me, legs folded like wings. The seminal stage of family is already pushing me aside. I dress and leave at dawn. Crows chase a barred owl caught in the sun's pink glow.

The opacity of fresh snowfall unfolds like a silent fan. The woodpile tarp is welded to the ground. I have begun to see pregnancy everywhere, the curve of a belly, the strain of release. Women give form to the language of life. Without them, men are mute. If fatherhood is compromise, then motherhood is sacrifice, an abandoning for the sacred, an act of heroism. Aztec women who died in childbirth went to the same exalted branch of heaven as warriors slain in battle.

Frontier women had an average of eight babies apiece before they were Rita's age, often ruining their bodies in the process. Many died young. It was not uncommon for men to marry again after wearing the first wife out. The notion of Rita's death petrifies me into five minutes of somnolence, staring at an oak. Strips of snow lie in the furrows of its striated bark. I don't know which would be worse—losing my mate or raising a child alone. The obvious answer pummels me with shame. My concerns for Rita's mortality have little to do with her. I want her alive to make life easier for me.

I release the oak beside the river or perhaps the oak releases me. Blizzard scraps from two weeks back lie in shade strips cast by trees. Breath is condensing to ice on my beard. The control of fire keeps us warm and separates us from animals more than the wheel. Our house sits on a stretch of river between two sharp curves. Sewage from town prevents these bends from freezing and bald eagles have begun to fish the open water. They scan the river from high limbs. Water gurgles like distant music beneath the river's lid of ice, bubbling through the slits.

A groundhog trail is easy to recognize by the dirt it leaves mixed with snow. My tracks are the most obvious, the tread of boots with a turned-out angle to the stride. They look clumsy beside the elegance of fox prints, the petite mouse trail, the smooth swath left by a beaver's tail. Rita took a brief walk last week and I studied her tracks. Most humans come down hard on a heel or toe. Hers were balanced, both ends of each foot sunk deep, as she rocked the weight forward and back. She is tired of the house, of winter, of being pregnant. She tells me the payoff is worth the aggravation. For her, birth is an end; for me, the beginning of deeper concern. I am no better at keeping jobs than I ever was. I've only gotten better at finding them.

Beaver saliva twinkles in fresh wood chips, and the air is still as a crypt. My crunching footsteps are very loud. The absence of leaves allows me to see farther in the woods than in any other season. Farmers call this weather an open winter—cold and windy, barren as Detroit or the Bronx, sightlines spreading in every direction. I can view my life without obstruction. Everything leads to this moment. An eagle watches me from a mile away.

There are various places in the woods that are special to me, each marking where something occurred on an earlier trip. Nothing distinguishes them save the ghost of memory. Today I am visiting these areas, as comfortable with them as with an old friend. I come to the spot where I stood last fall skipping rocks across the river. One of my stones struck a crappie that was jumping for an insect. The geometry was pure—arcing stone, flashing fish, the sudden collision that left me weak. I felt abandoned by logic, alone as paternity on the rise. Water rejected a rock. The air welcomed a fish.

Last night's sleet covers every twig and bole with glittering ice, changing each tree to a thousand prisms. Snowflakes float big as nickels. I'm walking a world that sparkles around me. The floor of the woods has hardened like old varnish. Squirrels scurry easily along the veneer, but my boots stay on top for a millisecond before weight and gravity break the crust. My mind slows to the cadence of the frost.

These are the woods of Poweshieck, chief of Mesquakie, the Red Earth People. The remainder of his tribe lives in Tama County now, north of here. Last year Rita and I attended a powwow held in the town's rec center. White families watched from bleachers as dancers competed beneath basketball goals. They wore costumes passed down through generations. The Mesquakie beat rhythms on a single drum, singing the songs of the past. After the last Indian quilt was raffled off, the white people began to leave the gym.

Bear and panther were eliminated in my grandfather's day, bobcat and wolf in my father's. The last passenger pigeon died a captive in 1914. None of us can ever see a sabertooth. In recent years, Old Faithful has lost its fidelity; the spew is erratic and short, the product of land rendered impotent by men. Our species is becoming Icarus with melting wax and loss of altitude. The sea will drink us. The air will breathe us. The soil will eat our mulch.

My boots drop through the brittle surface, and the snow becomes a powdery beach of the lost midwestern sea. The ocean has receded and I am walking with the dodo, the condylarth, the living trilobite. A jetty of land is an open coral reef. Instead of birds, there are feathered creatures learning to glide. I am the only animal on its hind legs, bewildered by the ability to grasp. I become conscious of the self, which marks the fearing of death, our fatal flaw. I wear store-bought hides, lack decent claws and teeth. My nose is ruined from breathing the air of cities, and I need binoculars to aid my vision. A mouse can outrun me with no head start.

I sit on a downed poplar where last spring I found a petrified bullfrog the size of a brick. Its skin was leathery black. The frog's posture was halted on the verge of a leap, with the bones of its rear legs making humps in its back. It smelled bad. I spoke to a biologist, who asked to see it. He said that last year thousands of frogs had suddenly died and people were concerned. After a couple of days, he called, disappointed that my frog's death was explainable. It had frozen to death. I hung up the phone thinking about our penchant for uncommon deaths—the woman who is struck by lightning, the worker who drowns in a brewery, the man whose final coronary happens when he is making love. Jesus died in an unusual fashion and we still have not gotten over it.

This morning's walk ends at a channel that links the river to several ponds. The ice is covered with fox prints in frozen blood, and the oily feathers of a duck. During last year's high water, I steered my boat up the channel at night and enjoyed the purity of being lost in darkness, surrounded by the calling of owl and frog. Fish also wander into this waterway. Its mouth becomes blocked by brush, and when the water recedes, the fish are trapped in the ponds that slowly dry to mud.

Just before Rita became pregnant, we found a gar halfway along this channel. It was working through mud toward the river. A quick slithering motion yanked its body forward a few inches, where it rested briefly. We stared at a fish on land, dragging itself like a wounded soldier into safe territory. Its sheer exertion was appalling.

The gar is ancient, a throwback with its tough hide and alligator snout filled with dozens of sharp teeth. It is a relentless predator. The eggs of a gar are poison to other fish, so it has not changed much in sixty-five million years. Rita suggested I help the fish, but I refused, preferring not to tamper with nature. Watching a fish on land was like finding a mermaid, farfetched and wondrous.

Rita plunged into the muddy trench, falling several times. The gar got away from her twice. She finally caught it on her knees and grinned at me, mud specking her teeth. The river flowed behind her. She and the gar were covered with muck. Both seemed to have risen simultaneously from the earth. The woods around me faded to a void. I skipped backwards several million years to an antediluvial age when earth and water were more closely connected, when there was less division between dwellers of each. All creatures aspired to the expansive qualities of the amphibian.

Today the mud is hard as clay beneath the snow and ice. I'll be a father by the time water returns to the channel. The baby is long past its fish stage. Eyes initially occur on the side of its head before slowly moving forward. We are descendants of a Devonian fish, but our arrival on land was due to a failure in water, not to innate superior skills. Dominant forms arise from the lowly, the least specialized, the quickest to adapt. Humans are the underclass of evolution. Every other creature was better equipped.

The curled leaves of a burr oak rasp one another in the wind. The sun is a white glow in the sky. While walking out, I see a bald eagle tuck its wings and drop from the sky like a meteor. At the last second it opens its wings to brake. The talons swing forward and back, shattering the placid surface of water, and the eagle climbs into the air clutching a fish. The vision so discombobulates me that I momentarily forget to breathe. The soaring bird becomes a speck that disappears in the glare of full sunrise.

Decades of DDT have weakened the eggshells of eagles until a female can kill her young merely by warming the eggs. I am stricken by a sudden fear that Rita will fall out of bed and crush the fetus. I hurry home, reminding myself that the placenta is stronger and more complex than a spacesuit. It girdles the baby as the earth once protected all of humanity.

Rita is smiling when I enter the house. Heat from the stove draws steam from my clothes. My face stings. I stare through a mist of my own making, unable to tell her how glad I am that she's alive. I mention the gar and she nods, her eyes elsewhere, inside. We both glance away. The winter of our intimacy has made us shy.

Shadrack was the first friend I'd had in years, and I decided to join him in Boston. He refused to take me in, saying I required too much psychic space. In Cambridge I interviewed with several "group houses" but my character betrayed me: I smoked, ate red meat, and was a Virgo—poor company to the enlightened. I dialed a number in a roommate tabloid and was interviewed at midnight by five insomniacs in Jamiaca Plain, known as J.P. They accepted me by unanimous decision, a fact that should have made me wary.

J.P. was considered one of Boston's bad neighborhoods, wedged into a slight gap between two worse neighborhoods. Renovated condos chipped the perimeter, the children of the white flight returning for revenge. The elevated orange line connected everyone by air. I lived near the Green Street station, an area I was often warned against. To protect myself, I wore a scarred leather jacket and a permanent scowl. While walking home one night, I watched a couple cross the street to avoid me, and half a block later cross back. It was one of the better moments of my urban life. I felt vindicated for the general apprehension I carried in the street.

The rooming house was a prewar blight waiting to be renovated and peddled floor by floor. A pair of nitwits who called themselves "urban pioneers" owned the building but lived in fancy Back Bay. A Puerto Rican family lived on the ground floor. The father, Romero, raised chickens in the backyard, and was the manager of the building. He could kick us out at whim, a terrible prospect because when a man finds himself living in a rooming house, there is no place left to go.

Six of us shared a moldy bathroom and a rat-infested kitchen.

One guy ran a bankrupt construction business out of the hallway. All day and night his employees drifted around, young Israelis and Irish with no papers. They waited for work in the living room, comparing wars and scars, unified by hunger, cold, and exile. I've never seen Jews and Christians get along better.

I hooked a job at the Lune Café as the only waiter for lunch. The small room contained nine tables, revolutionary posters, and an organic menu. The cook was an antique hippie who held himself off the floor by one arm pretzeled through elastic legs. He grunted his name, Orion, while attaining nirvana beside the stove. A scrawny woman of forty emerged from the basement. She told me she was in therapy and believed that all psychologists should wash dishes. It was better than tofu or primal screaming.

"I've washed plenty," I said.

Dazzled by a sympathetic audience, she ranted for twenty minutes about the collective healing power of woman. She told me that the earliest Chinese ideograph for "male" also meant "selfish." Orion unfolded and shape-shifted to a full headstand. His shirt fell open to reveal a belly tattoo of the Aztec Sunstone radiating from his navel. He remained inverted until J.P.'s lunch rush. White boys with dreadlocks sprawled across two tables. Men wore earrings; the women shaved their heads. Conversation was tense and urgent. A guy with no hands ordered a salad and ate it like an animal while reading the *Daily Worker*.

Orion folded each order into soggy sheafs of papyrus that passed for bread in honor of repressed peoples. A customer demanded to know the contents of each item, including the precise amount of spice. His voice was nasal.

"One pinch or two of thyme?" he asked.

"I don't know," I said. "Are you allergic?"

"No," came the smug reply. "I am macro."

Later Orion drew intricate charts to explain a macrobiotic diet. Hitler ate no meat, but vegetarians are reluctant to accept him as their own. West Point won't claim Benedict Arnold, and Kentuckians hate to admit that Charlie Manson was a native. No matter where you go, everyone says he's from the next county over.

For the next several weeks I lived on raisins, hummus, tempeh, and rice. I lost weight. My nose ran like a sieve. I fell victim to hamburger cravings that Orion deemed a stopover along the path to enlightenment. The dishwasher quit to join a commune of women attempting isolation from men. She suggested I interview as a possible sperm donor because my kundalini was halfway along my chakras.

One morning I woke with an absolute revulsion for work. Determined to get fired, I skipped a shower and wore a plastic nose-and-glasses the entire shift. During the rush, I removed my shirt and pants, wearing only undershorts, a white apron, and the giant nose. People left enormous tips. Someone asked what band I played with. Enraged by my unprecedented failure to get fired, I ripped a sacred Che Guevara poster from the wall and folded it into a hat.

At three o'clock I quit, leaving a squad of neo-anarchists arguing the Spanish civil war over cinnamon espresso. Safely outside, I felt relief tingle my skin. Quitting a job was the last way I had to prove the existence of my own free will. I began planning my return to New York City. Manhattan and Eastern Kentucky both operated from a social anarchy that I could negotiate with ease and comfort. When Gandhi was asked what he thought of Western civilization, he replied that it would be a good idea.

I headed into the Combat Zone, where mobilization had replaced the shooting galleries and brothels. Junkies poked their arms inside a car window for a quick injection. Pimps drove vans with a mattress in the back and a whore up front. She opened the passenger door to display her wares, and if a guy liked the sight, he entered the van for a quick transaction while the pimp casually circled the block.

For economy's sake I chose the bar with the most broken bulbs on its neon sign. The Minotaur's door opened to the damp smell of musk and beer. A rotating mirror ball flicked bright specks onto a stage that held a jukebox smeared with greasy fingerprints. I chugged a beer as a woman plodded the stage, watching herself in the mirrored walls. A bruise marred her inner thigh. She seemed bored. The bartender argued with an old man holding a raincoat over his spindly lap. Finally he pulled the coat away, exposing not his genitals but a colostomy bag.

A woman squeezed beside me, rubbing warm breasts against my arm. A python twined her shoulder and arm, its tiny tongue licking the air. She was a human caduceus in charge of ailing men.

"What's your snake's name?" I yelled above the raucous music.

"Boots."

"Good name."

"He's only the size of a belt, but he'll grow."

"That was Caligula's childhood nickname."

"Who?"

"Caligula."

"Does he come in here?"

I shook my head.

"If anyone tries to make boots from Boots," she said, "I'll fucking kill them."

Back room action cost fifty bucks, plus a twenty-five-dollar bottle of champagne to assure the club its cut. She said I could use a credit card. I had a two-dollar lingam and had no choice but to leave, feeling guilty, as if I'd rejected her good intentions. I told her I'd be back later, not wanting her to know I was broke.

Outside, the air was different from a change in weather, one of the coast's wily tricks. The sky was a gray flannel blanket like a watercolor background with too much paint. Wind blew trash along the gutter. Dusk raised a full moon that looked as if it could be peeled away to leave a knothole in the sky. The moon was full as a tick, the mark of lunacy.

I recalled a man I'd known in New York who'd been lobotomized during the 1950s. He'd gone to Islip, Long Island, where the procedure was so popular that the town was nicknamed

"Icepick." Fifteen years later he was released from an institution and placed in my neighborhood. I once watched him trying to cross a busy intersection. He took two steps forward and one back, his movements never varying. He swung his arms and tilted his head, and on each forward step, he'd say, "Green light. The light's green."

There was a mechanized element to his movements, as with a movie actor playing an android. I realized that the front of his head was short-circuiting and he was caught in a synaptic repetition, like faulty wiring that blows the same fuse each time you flick the light switch. I took his arm and said, "Come on, let's go."

Immediately the circuitry righted itself.

"Thank you," he said. "I'm going for coffee, for coffee."

Dusting Jamaica Plain were various artists living illegally in warehouses without plumbing. Shadrack had a studio a few blocks from the rooming house, and used my shower on Tuesday or Thursday. He had a few stops around town, all charted on a pocket calendar from last year. The true dates didn't matter since the days of the week never changed. On a particularly lonesome day I called him at noon, rousting him from sleep. He grunted twice and whined a litany of woe. One of his girlfriends might be pregnant, his paintings were terrible, and his bowels had failed him three days running. Believing his troubles more genuine than mine, I was momentarily cheered.

An hour later Shadrack arrived for a shower. He griped about the dullness of my razor, and demanded a pair of socks. He was angry that I had not washed the only towel that I owned.

"It's been three months," he said.

"Bring your own, Shad."

"How can you live like that?"

"I don't get as dirty as you."

"Good point," he said. "But I have to stay clean for the women."

"The young one, the rich one, or the one who might be pregnant?"

He stared at me, insulted. His correction came low and firm. "They are all rich."

He dressed and left. Shadrack's dates were invariably white and blond, the angular descendants of northern Europe. He didn't mind their eating disorders, their stabbing hipbones, their preoccupation with the clothes of other women. When I suggested variety, he refused on the grounds that his mother had dark hair and eyes. As soon as the right trust fund appeared, he would catapult from a heatless warehouse to a skylit studio in SoHo. Until then, he'd make do with my shower.

Under Shadrack's influence, I hit upon my most ingenious artistic thought—to write a poem about a specific object, then transcribe it onto the object itself. The first priority was to find suitable junk. I spent hours wandering in alleys, seeking industrial trash. My journal filled with entries about a planned gallery show of "found-object-poetry." I jammed my room with detritus, but never quite got around to writing any poems.

One of the boarders left the rooming house, and Shadrack recommended a woman who worked at a bakery. She'd bring home free food, which I was to share with him as a finder's fee. Diana was a three-hundred-pound, toothless native of Maine, my age and height, built like a sumo wrestler with silo thighs. She always wore a battered bicycle helmet with rearview mirrors like insect feelers. The day we met, she lacked front teeth. A bicycle hung carelessly over one immense shoulder.

"Hi, Chrith. My upper plate ith at the dentitht. Where can I keep my bike?"

"Anywhere's fine. Nothing really matters here."

"I know. That'th why I'm here. Thadrack thaid you're a poet."

"How'd you lose your teeth?"

"Knocked out in a poolroom."

"Uh, yeah. Make yourself at home, Diana. I've got to do some serious writing."

Safe in my room, I lay in bed and drank a finger's width of

bourbon, pleased that Shadrack considered me a poet. It was a sign that our friendship was solid, since I'd still written nothing. Wittgenstein suggested that the truly sacred was ineffable, that the unsaid was more important than the said. As proof, he renounced all of his teachings. I was trying to go him one step further, increase the purity of my eloquence by refusing to write at all, rather than merely abandoning the practice. Anyone could quit. It required real courage never to begin.

Every morning, Diana trudged from her room wearing a tattered red robe ripped at the seams to reveal acres of flesh. She bummed cigarette after cigarette. During childhood, she confided, the other kids slipped razor blades in apples and threw them at her.

"Diana," I finally said. "Go put your plate in your mouth."

She returned to fix a cup of Maine coffee. After filling a sock with beans, she smashed them with a pan and dropped the sock in boiling water. The resulting muck could float a bullet. The recipe was from her father, an alcoholic who beat his wife, children, and livestock when drunk. He died of multiple snakebite wounds after passing out in a nest. Diana was fourteen years old and weighed two-twenty. She told me she'd gained weight deliberately, hoping to make herself ugly enough to halt her father's visits to her bedroom.

"I never told a man that before, Chris."

"Uh, yeah," I said. "I'm glad you trust me."

She grabbed my shoulders and clubbed me in a hug that ripped her red robe further. One sleeve dangled like a hammock from shoulder to wrist. This rite of camaraderie cemented us enough for her lover to move in.

Young and attractive, Sophia endeared herself to me with her habitual breakfast of diced garlic mixed in plain yogurt. She explained that any foulness in her body fled the garlic. Sophia was always chipper, never sick, and to my knowledge, was unbothered by vampires. Her passage through the hall left a vapor. One evening I came home to find Diana pacing a ragged circle in the kitchen, a fierce expression on her face. Sophia slumped in a chair.

"She got fired," Sophia said.

"So what," I said.

"She knocked her boss out first."

"He made fun of my weight," Diana said. "So I cold-cocked him."

I rummaged my room for a pint of Kentucky's finest and passed it around. Diana knocked back a two-bubble drink.

"Thanks, Chris. I stayed until he came to. That's when he fired me. I said I was sorry. He was too embarrassed to press charges."

I invited Diana to battle an old boss from Salem, a beefy Frenchman who might last a couple of rounds. She refused because her invariable triumph won no friends.

"Men can fight and be buddies afterwards," she explained. "But a woman who whips a man is always a bull dyke."

"You're no dyke," Sophia slurred. "You're a sweetie pie."

Diana slapped me on the back.

"I'm a lucky buckaroo. This one thinks I'm special."

"She's just drunk."

Diana laughed and laughed. I handed her the bottle. She finished it and dropped her fists to splayed knees.

"For a man," she said, "you're a good hombre."

They staggered into their room. That night and thereafter, Sophia and Diana left their bedroom door open while making love, a gleeful concert that encased the house in guttural sound. One stuttered a banshee keen while the other snorted and moaned. The jamboree mounted to a dual crescendo of high screams before fading to a gurgle. Encores followed for hours. Night after night I felt a certain reverence for their endurance. They seemed completely uninhibited and free from the recuperative needs of a man. Though neither attracted me, I was jealous of their mutual delight.

Sophia refused to seek employment, claiming that she wouldn't succumb to the patriarchal system. Diana took a job at a car wash. One afternoon Sophia asked if I'd ever had a homosexual experience. I shook my head, remembering men in New York who'd cruised me with such diligence that I'd begun to wonder if they recognized some latent quality that I didn't know about. A kindly old man finally explained that men were simply more aggressive than women, that I should view male attention as nothing more than a compliment. "Do you look at women on the street?" he asked.

I nodded.

"Well," he said, "fags look at men the same way. If you're gay, you know it. But don't wait until you're fifty to come out of the closet. There's nothing worse than an old queen. I couldn't get laid in prison."

Two of my past girlfriends had been involved with women. Another had hoped to sleep with a woman as an "empowering experience." I told Sophia about them and she explained that our society was a dinosaur shuffling toward calamity. We'd betrayed Mother Earth, a bitter old woman who'd married out of faith. I told her that Appalachians didn't fit that category.

"We did a unit on you," she said.

"What?"

"In school. Advanced Sociology. You're oppressed, you know."

"No I'm not. I left."

"Good for you. That's like coming out of the closet."

"Not exactly."

"I think you've got some lesbian in you, Chris. You're like a sister to Diana and me."

"What time is it? I have to go find a job."

"You just think you have to. It's conditioning. No woman should wash dishes for a living."

"I'm a man."

"Yeah, I guess so."

I left, considering her idea. Perhaps she was right, and the miasmic flow of my life was merely stress from being a lesbian trapped inside a man's body. I could save money and have a sex change.

Then I could surrender to the narcissism of loving that which I was—a woman.

When spring arrived we opened the windows, a mistake that cost our idyllic life. The sound of Sophia and Diana's amorous uproar carried into the neighborhood. Just after the peak of their joy one night, a banging began at the front door. I crossed the kitchen and greeted Romero fidgeting in his long johns.

"You have trouble here," he said, glancing past me to scan the kitchen.

"No trouble. Everything's fine."

"I hear all week a woman being beat. That is not fine. Not every night."

"Really, Romero. It's okay."

"Where is the big one?"

"Do you think I could beat her?"

"And the other? She lives here now?"

"No. She's a friend."

"Of who?"

"She's my girlfriend."

Romero closed his eyes, aware of my lie, face pained with disappointment.

"She must go. Both of them. One month."

He shook his head and descended the narrow stairs, a successful immigrant bamboozled by America.

I informed Diana over morning coffee. Her entire head became red. She walked to her room and calmly tore the door from its hinges. Ten minutes later she left, abandoning everything she owned, a decision I respected.

Snugly unemployed, I developed an eating system at the faithful Lune Café. I sauntered in every day for organic gruel and gave Orion a five-dollar bill. Pretending to make change, he handed me the five, plus four ones. I left the singles for a tip and kept the five. He called it exploiting the oppressor. All spring the same five bucks bought lunch, often my only meal.

I came home to learn that Shadrack had showered while I was gone. My towel was missing. I called to ask him about it.

"Get a new one," he said.

"I only need one."

"It's more sanitary to have a couple."

"For who, you or me?"

"The world, Chris. You have to think in terms of global health."

"Well, I've got one more towel than you do."

"Not anymore."

He agreed to return the towel if I bought him a beer. We met at a bar and conversation steered unerringly to suicide. Shadrack believed that talking about it prevented the occurrence, by "keeping it in the world, not in my head."

"Why keep the idea alive at all?" I said.

"You're missing the point. Suicide is for people who care about life. Mine doesn't matter. First I'll get a hot-air balloon and set it up with one rope tying it to the ground. The balloon is a circle seen from any direction. The perfect mandala. I'll hang a noose from the bottom and put my head in. Then I'll cut the anchor line. The flight strangles me in the air."

"What about a note?"

"That's pinned to my chest. It says, 'Bury me where I land.' "

"Like Robin Hood's arrow."

"Not bad, huh? I need two video cameras, one on the ground and one in the balloon. My final work of art. It'll start a movement. I'll be famous."

"Is this a threat because I want my towel back?"

"Relax. Planning all the details keeps it at bay, like a jar of pennies when you're broke. You know what I worry about? That suicide just puts things off. You don't die, you just wander after the living like a deaf Pied Piper."

"Your superstition is showing."

"What do you mean?"

"Purgatory."

THE SAME RIVER TWICE

"Did you know that comes from the word 'purge'?"

Half listening to his lecture on the etymology of death, I looked around the murky bar lined by sad faces atop sagging bodies. Perched on the last stool beside the door was a patient hooker sipping sweet drinks. She didn't look bad.

"Painting is a waste," Shadrack said. "I think I'll quit and join a Trappist monastery. It's the same as suicide except you have to live. Know what I mean, Chris?"

"Nope."

"The vow of silence."

"I wouldn't mind if you took that."

"I'm serious. I should go to India and steal a cart so they'll cut my hands off. That way I can't make things, the vow of visual silence."

"Why don't you start with a finger," I said.

"Why don't you write a poem!"

"Maybe I took a vow."

"I think you're scared."

"The only thing I'm scared of is snakes."

"Look, Chris. You better start writing or you'll wind up like me."

The words had flowed without prior thought and I watched their meaning seep into him. Shadrack seemed to shrivel. Very slowly he pushed his beer glass off the table. It shattered against the floor. There was deliberation in the act, rather than violence; the careful work of controlled passion. He leaned across the table, his voice a hard whisper.

"That's poetry, my friend. That's how you write it."

He handed me the towel as if he were a master of tae kwon do granting a star pupil the highest belt.

"Now leave me alone," he said. "Go write."

The bartender walked over and I apologized, offered to pay for the glass. Shadrack was gone and I hadn't seen him leave. We'd argued before, often mightily, but this time there was a finality to his calm. I thought about our past conversations, his view of the artist as shaman. He considered the process of making art to be holy. Shadrack had given me permission and now he was gone.

During the next nine weeks, I faced my typewriter and never wrote a word. I rolled a fresh page into the machine and stared like a statue for fifteen hours. At the day's end I placed the blank page to the right of my typewriter. My mind was a tornado. I ceased to bathe, eat, or shave. I simply continued to write without writing.

My brain began to operate in a lucid fashion, seeing details of memory melting into dialogue. I was invigorated by the electrical crossfire in my head. On particularly luminous days, my brain pulsed in a state of ecstasy. The moment I awoke, I rushed to use it, sliding into the marvelous oblivion of self-content, flowing with the same aimless delight of hitchhiking. My mind entered the blank white page to observe myself: a thin skin bag over a fragile gantry of bone. Cartilage hinged the moving parts.

Mail ruined my discipline, bringing a birthday card from my mother. Without quite noticing, I had become thirty years old. I went out for a pint of bourbon, drank it too fast, and got sick. I was in that panting, sweaty state when men swore off alcohol, bargained with God, and resolved to hold a job. I had done it many times. Though I refused to admit failure, I was certainly engaged in failing. The time had come to squirrel a grubstake and leave Boston.

I called the personnel office at the Grand Canyon and was told that the hiring was over, but that I should try the Everglades. It had a late season. I called Flamingo, Florida, and reached a man named Bucky. He said there was an opening for a Naturalist.

"What are your qualifications?" he asked.

"I grew up in the woods."

"Well, we need a tour guide. Ours had an accident. Have you been down here before?"

"Sure," I lied.

"I'll pick you up in Florida City. Call me when you get there. I need a break from this swamp."

I bought a book about South Florida and spent the evening looking at photographs of paradise. Every animal native to North America lived there. The Everglades seemed like Kentucky with alligators and a beach.

The night before leaving, I nailed my towel to the door of Shadrack's studio, with a note telling him my plans. I decided to celebrate with a drink at one of Boston's slickest bars. The acrylic stools were shaped like swans. On one wall hung a liquor poster urging "the art of lingering." Cooking, war, and flower arrangement had all been elevated to the status of art, and it occurred to me that the high arts had responded by demoting themselves to craft. I decided this was why I wasn't writing.

I went home and filled a glass with bourbon and frothing tap water. The alcohol killed the chlorine that killed the germs. This was a good old day. In New England I had no more found America than Columbus had. He died obscure, humiliated, and a trifle cracked. His bones were dug up three times, finally ensconced in a lighthouse in the Dominican Republic. At the tip of Florida, I'd be fairly close.

I rode the commuter train to I-95, a straight shot to Florida. Boston faded into morning smog—Bunker Hill's phallic monument that commemorated the wrong neighborhood, the icy sliver of the Hancock building, a harbor full of poison. My backpack contained spare clothes and a blank notebook with the word "Poetry" scrawled on the cover. Ponce de León had grown old traipsing Florida for the Fountain of Youth; perhaps I could find the Well of Age.

Half a dozen pillows prop Rita's swollen body on the couch. The woman I married has been replaced by an incubator with powers of speech and thought. A blithering numbskull has replaced her husband. Our sole heat is a woodstove that warms the ceiling and leaves pockets of cold in the corners. Ice has formed on the windows inside the house. The baby has dropped. Its head is positioned correctly, nudging Rita's pelvic exit. Her belly has tilted forward and she breathes more easily, but the change in her center of gravity affects her balance. She moves like a drunk. I scatter salt from the door to the car. It melts through snow in hundreds of tiny pocks.

After agreeing easily to a girl's name, Rebecca Marie, we fought over what to call a boy. I want a common name that is still uncommon, an older name, one of strength, such as Oak or Thor. Rita eschews my ideas as ridiculous. Her names are fine, Ben, Jared, Lucas, but I didn't think of them first. We make lists, writing each name on an index card, granting the other power of veto. It is like choosing a jury; we both add token names to our list for the other to deny. The rest go into separate stacks of yes, no, and maybe. The no pile is the biggest.

My father and brother share the same name, being the fifth and the sixth respectively. If we have a boy, both have urged me to use their name, continuing a line that runs to the Civil War. Rita's father would prefer us to name a boy after his brother who died in World War II. The name is Jack, which does not jibe with my last name. Before I understood the meaning, I engaged in grade school fistfights with boys who called me that. When I make fun of the name, Rita begins to weep. After all, it is her dead uncle I'm laughing at. I apologize and prowl the house like a caged animal until she sends me to the woods.

Morning shadows are blue in the snow. Winter is a bell, a long peal of silence through the floodplain woods. Every horizontal surface is blanked white and my bad knee aches. The river is frozen along the bank, forming a white border for its flow. The ice on both sides slowly meets in the middle, joining like Rita and me on a name. The center of the river is the first to thaw. It gradually breaks itself until it reaches the shore, leaving silver shelves of ice protruding from the bank.

The woods are black and white, like an old photograph. I know the names of trees but they are only words. The Sac Indians said that *kaintuck* meant "river of blood." According to them, Eastern Kentucky was filled with the ghosts of its previous inhabitants, an ancient race slaughtered to the last child. The Sac were astonished that white people would want to homestead the hills. The name itself prevented their own people from living there.

The oldest recorded personal name is En-lil-ti, carved into a Sumerian tablet from 3300 B.C. "Rita" is a Sanskrit word, meaning "brave" or "honest." My name means "bearer of Christ," a troublesome burden. When I was a child, Saint Christopher was removed from sainthood and I thought that meant he was bad, that I was impugned by his inadequacy. I decided to change my name but the family objected. Unbound by such fetters, a Hindu will choose a new name to mark significant personal change. Cherokee people may change their names several times to suit their personalities at different stages of life. I want a son's name to suit him so well he'll want it for life.

At the river's edge I begin tracking a deer. The prints are coming my way, which means I'm not following the deer but trailing it in reverse, going where it came from. The snow inside each print is compacted but loose, a fresh trail. I find where the animal ducked a low branch, knocking snow from the bough. I duck under it too. The tree limb brushes my back as it brushed the deer. The tracks end on a slight rise forty yards from the river at a spot that is protected from wind. An oval swatch of earth is imprinted in the snow. The deer slept here last night, melting the snow beneath it. I've found where it sleeps, giving me a power as ancient as knowing a wizard's name.

I crouch at the perimeter and retrieve a few lost hairs. They are
stiff bristles an inch long, two of which are tipped in white. I push
them into my beard and lie in the bed of the deer. Its heavy musk
clings to the dirt, full of mystery and strength. In the fifth century,
Parmenides said, "All things are a name where mortals lie down."
The bottoms of trees fill my vision, becoming a solid wall in the
distance. I pull into a tighter ball. The ground is cold against my
face. I try to imagine sleeping through the darkness here, comfortable with the sounds of night, waking at first light. Tree limbs
interlace around me, edged with snow that's white as milk.

In olden times, women gave the children names, an act connected
with lactation. Eating was evidence of life, and life demanded a
label. Since the men didn't nurse, they were excluded from the
process of naming. French women still give infants a milk name, a
temporary appellation while the child is nursing. This name embod-
ies the soul and is kept secret. Inuit society requires a three-day
waiting period before naming a newborn. They want to examine it
first, ensure that its presence is acceptable to the community. Until
the baby is named, it is not considered human.

I realize that I'm quite cold. My weak knee throbs, my bad ear
aches. I haven't been lying here very long and already I'm uncomfortable. The recognition of such simple failure is worse than my
fears of being a lousy father. I uncurl and rise, moving through the
timber. Wind off the river scorches my face. I think of Adam, the
unremitting pressure of naming every creature. Each word he uttered became a noun.

A beaver-downed tree spreads its branches along the ice where
the river touches land. The current carries hundreds of small fish
along the surface. Most are dead, but a few still struggle with feeble
fins. A dozen float in a pool formed by a beaver dam, and I wonder
if they are of the same spawn, born and dying together. I imagine
being in the woods with my children, and realize that I'm already
thinking in the plural, although we have yet to name the first. The
baby Rita carries will need an ally against me. A backup prevents

extinction. This need for another name reduces the pressure of choosing one now. Like Adam, I have room for error.

More dead fish are floating by, tiny and silver, the shape of a spearpoint. Life will divide siblings as surely as a dam divides the river. The Hindu goddess Bindumati parted the Ganges, and Isis divided the Phaedras River. Moses came late to the myth. He suffered a speech impediment and relied on his brother's eloquence until they entered the wilderness and began to disagree. Thinking of Aaron's magic rod, I use a forked stick to lift a fish from the river. A black spot behind each eye marks it as a gizzard shad, a fragile creature that cannot sustain sudden changes in temperature. Thousands die every year, entire clans wiped out. Our child will never have a big brother or sister, nor wear hand-me-downs. I place the shad on the log for a possum or coon. Nothing dies before its time.

Beneath the snow is a layer of last fall's leaves, and walking it is like treading upon a mattress. The ground is marked by deer print and droppings. I remove my glove and squeeze a pellet between thumb and forefinger. It's soft, still warm. I'm close.

When I stop at the edge of a clearing, a deer lifts its head to watch me with the bold curiosity of a raccoon. Direct eye contact is a sign of aggression that will scare most animals, and I turn my head, looking to the side of the deer. We share the gift of acknowledgment. It will outwait me because there is no time in the woods, only life and rot, with weather at the edges. I have never owned a watch. Time is a Rorschach folded into a Möbius strip turned inside out, upside down. Time is the name we give to living. Modern science presents us with kingdom, phylum, class, order, family, genus, and species—designating every organism on the planet. Once identified, it is ours, as with a nickname known only to a private few. Quantum physics has taken to naming the theoretical, much like concocting a name for an unborn infant. Nothing exists that is not labeled; like killing, it is our assertion over the world.

The deer I'm watching moves to nibble a branch, accustomed to my shape among the trees and brush. Something immobile is not a threat. The deer looks back at me occasionally and I imagine that it recognizes its fur in my beard. My cheek begins to itch but I refuse to scratch it and drive the deer to flight. Many eons ago, the name was identical with the thing itself, a method of comprehension. The word "deer" comes from the Old English "deor," meaning "beast." Gradually the word moved from the general to the specific. A beast became the deer. The present denudes the past.

In Sanskrit, *naman* means both "name" and "soul." Dogs, cats, and horses receive our patronizing gift of a name because they knuckle under us. My mother talks to her houseplants and gives them names. Language protects us, the foremost tool of the weakest mammal. To name is to know, the first step of identity. One child, one name; the grafting of the soul.

A crow angles into a hickory and perches with its bill parted, a young bird's habit from the nest, waiting for food. When I turn my head to look at it, the deer flees, tail raised like a flag of surrender. Its abrupt flight startles me. I sense its fear, a feeling that I fill with my own sudden panic. I hurry across the hardened earth, certain that Rita is giving birth.

My panting entrance to the house awakens her on the couch. She's had no contractions. The baby has dropped, but its head has not yet engaged, still floating in its private amniotic river. I bring Rita juice and sit beside her, waiting like the crow for the sustenance of life. We settle on a name. If it's a boy, we'll call it Sam and worry about the particulars later.

Rita stretches her arms for a hug, breasts swollen, hair silken on my face. The smell of fresh-split white oak fills the house. We lie on the couch all day, watching early darkness cloud the air. I press my belly against hers, feel the baby move. The moon hangs round and white as a fresh tree stump. I feed the fire, knowing that our child's birth will drive a velvet wedge between us. We're less lovers than partners now, old buddies facing weather, followers of habit. We've spread our wings and mated for life. She has taken my name.

Two days after leaving Boston, I slept beneath a picnic table at a rest stop in Grizzard, Virginia. My body was stiff but I felt an adrenalized state of grace. The crammed sprawl of the Northeast lay behind me. I was bound for the southernmost tip of continental America, a gigantic swamp, a river of grass. I decided to give up alcohol and dope. The Everglades would be my detox center, a monastery. I was certain to live there the rest of my life.

An independent trucker stopped because he needed someone to keep him awake. Twenty hours later he dropped me off just south of Jacksonville, where I watched hundreds of drivers cruise along I-95 without so much as glancing my way. I walked several miles to the intersection of A1A and found a message on a road sign. Scratched into the shiny metal back, as if by a dying man writing his own epitaph, were these words: "Worst place in USA to get a ride. 3 days here. Fuck Florida. Fritz."

Below that ran an equally chilling ledger of the road:

3 days—Will
27 hours—Schmitty
17 hours—Larry
2½ days—Pablo
32 hours—Phil
1 day, 4 hours, 18 minutes—Pete the Tick

At the very bottom of the sign, carved with a wavering hand, was the finale: "You're stuck, brother. Kick back, smoke dope, get high."

Until a few thousand years ago, Florida was under water, making it the world's most recent substantial landmass to emerge. Reading that sign made me wish it had remained in the sea. The lovely resort town of Flamingo was better than four hundred miles away. I decided to buck the odds, trust whichever goddess watched over vagrants and swamplands, and hang my thumb to the wind. To dodge the sun, I stood in the sliver of shadow cast by the sign. Seven hours later I was still there, bug-chewed, delirious from the heat, facing the flip side of freedom—the numb despair of immobility.

Nine miles east lay the ocean, an eternity of light-years away. The rest of the continent spread above me like a fan. I realized that I had no idea what I was up to, in fact never had. Twelve years after leaving Kentucky, I was still roving the twentieth century, ineluctably alone and no better at it, merely accustomed to the circumstance. The West was fenced, Everest climbed, and Africa plumbed. Even Tibet had white men moving through it like a plague. Thumbing was a pathetic substitute for adventure. As a young man, I'd found this means of travel ideal, but now I was thirty, beyond the excuse of youth. For the first time in my life, I felt aged.

I crossed the highway, turned north, and was picked up by an old fisherman hauling a tin skiff in a pickup. The back third of the boat hung from the truck. He made me sit in the boat. As soon as we crossed into Georgia, I banged on the window and hopped out. He gave me half a can of bug spray, the most useful gift I've ever received. By dawn, the can was empty and I no longer bothered to scratch the bites that covered my body. The flesh around my eyes was swollen to blindness. When I staggered from the brush, two college boys stopped their car. They seemed disappointed that I was a victim of insects rather than a dope deal gone sour. Out of pity they allowed me passage to Florida.

In Miami I caught a bus to Florida City. The driver spoke no English, which explained why so many New Yorkers moved there—they felt at home. Florida City was the last town before the Everglades, and I wondered vaguely how I'd ever get out of Flamingo once I reached it. Wet air sopped against me like a sponge. I went to the bus station and called Bucky, who said he was on his way. An old man chewing snuff sat behind the ticket counter. I told him I was going to the Everglades. He unleashed a stream of tobacco that spattered a stained wall.

"No you ain't," he said.

"I got a job there."

"You ain't going there."

"Why not?"

"You're in the Glades already."

I went outside to wait for Bucky. From the edge of town, the monotonous landscape of saw grass and sedge spread in every direction, devoid of humanity's imprint. Above the low treeline was a pale gray sky. A mosquito bit me. Gradually and then in a rush I realized that the manner in which I'd been hired was unusual. As the humidity collided with my body and dampened my clothes, I wondered if coming to Florida in August was somewhat of an error. I had sixty dollars in my sock, enough to get somewhere else. I studied my map. With Lake Okeechobee as its eye, Florida looked like a turtle poking its head from the shell of America. From another angle, the state resembled a scarred and flaccid lingam, and I was headed for its tip. The wrinkled map was horribly familiar. If I left, I didn't know where to go. I'd lived in or passed through most of the country already.

A short, stocky man in a cowboy hat parked his truck at the curb.

"God double damn," he said. "Civilization! Are you Chris?"

I nodded. He studied my swollen face.

"Well, you don't look too natural for a Naturalist."

Bucky handed me a can of mosquito repellent and we drove twenty miles along a narrow blacktop road that wound through clumps of mangrove and endless saw grass. He pointed out landmarks that were little more than bumps—Mahogany Hammock, Long Pine Key, a scenic overlook that was three feet high. Snakes lay in the road, drawing warmth from the tar. Huge birds flashed overhead.

The road opened into the most pathetic outpost erected since Ponce de León's first camp. Flamingo's main building had two stories with an open breezeway overlooking the bay. Below that lay a dock. Strung along the coast was a succession of low ratty cabins, each having settled into the soft earth at a different pitch and yaw. Bucky sprayed himself with repellent, opened the truck, and ran to the nearest door.

Though it was daylight, there was no one in sight and no cars in the lot. A pulley clanked on a naked flagpole. I had the feeling that reality had slipped: I'd been slaughtered on the interstate and this was a particularly malevolent form of afterlife. When I left the truck, a squad of mosquitoes found my neck and face. I ran to the mysterious door, jerked it open, and stumbled inside.

"Jeezum Crow," Bucky said. "Don't let the swamp in."

He slammed the door and we spent the next couple of minutes killing mosquitoes. He gave me an official Naturalist shirt, the price of which would come out of my pay. He assigned me a room, and told me the employee dining hours. Room and board would also be deducted. I asked if we got paid in scrip, but he didn't get the joke.

"You missed supper," Bucky said. "See Captain Jack after breakfast."

"Where is everybody?"

"Who?"

"Anybody."

"No tourists today. The employees stay mostly indoors." He shook my hand. "Welcome to the swamp."

I got my pack and ran to my room, sustaining several bites while working the key. There was a dank bathroom, two double beds, and a sliding glass door that offered a ground-level view of the ocean a hundred yards away. Wet air stifled the room and mildew grew in the corners. I turned on the air conditioner, which pumped a weak stream of warm air.

I unpacked and began to read the Florida book, rather than merely looking at the photographs as I had in Boston. Altitude was measured in inches. The fruit of the manchineel tree was water-soluble and so extremely toxic that taking shelter from rain beneath its boughs would poison you. I had voluntarily entered the most hostile environment known to man. Ponce de León had spent most of his time on the island of Bimini, and now I understood why.

A consistent banging woke me at dawn. Bucky stepped inside wearing a bathrobe, cowboy hat, and boots.

"Can you cook?" he said.

I shook my head.

"Know anybody who can?"

"I just got here."

"Right, right, the Naturalist. Forget breakfast, the cook quit. The boat's broke down, so there's no work for you today. Lucky bastard."

The *Heron* was a flat-bottomed scow with ten rows of benches beneath an awning. In the morning light that filtered through mist rising from the swamp, the boat looked as seaworthy as a brick. The hull showed a thick covering of algae and scum that clung like tattered lace to the wood. I'd traveled sixteen hundred miles to love my boat, planning to call it "she," and found the crone of the triple goddess. The most one could say of the *Heron* was that she might not leak.

A motorcycle honcho named Dirt concluded that to fix the motor, he'd have to pull it from the boat. I offered to help. We balanced the motor on the wide rail of the boat and began inching it onto the pier. Lateral pressure pushed the boat away from the dock. Dirt howled and I released the motor, which dropped into the dark green Florida Bay. Dirt spun to me, his face twitching at various spots. I backed away and he slammed his fist several times into the bridge.

For the next three hours Dirt sat slumped in the stern, staring overboard at the place where the motor had sunk. Each time I moved from the bow, he looked at me with such rage that I returned to my post and fought mosquitoes. Finally Bucky arrived, grinning like a frog.

"Fuck that motor," he said to Dirt. "I've already got a new one on order. Be here in a week."

"You fuck the motor," Dirt said. "I loved that thing."

"Damn good motor, Dirt. Damn good. You hungry?"

"Rafe come back?"

"Got over his titty-fit in Miami and came running back to Slim." Bucky looked at me. "They're Latin homos."

When I didn't answer, an expression of chagrin passed rapidly across his face. "Don't mean to offend you if you're one," he said.

"I'm not."

"Don't matter either way. Slim's worthless but Rafe used to cook in Havana. Got to take the hen to keep the drake."

After lunch, I learned that Flamingo had no beach. The land seemed neither to end nor the ocean begin, but at some imperceptible point one became the other in a fusion that shifted its boundary depending upon the tide. Mosquitoes hunted in great dark clouds. Tiny print on the can of repellent warned that the spray would corrode plastic, ruin varnish, and should not be ingested by humans. I limited its use to my clothes and sustained an average of a hundred and fifty bites per day. I soon developed something of an immunity.

While waiting for the new motor, I met a few of my fellow workers. Rafe and Slim were part of Castro's mass prison release of sociopaths and infidels. Slim told me that he loved Cuba for setting him free, and hated America for sending him to wash dishes in a swamp. Rafe pinned curlers to his hair, shaved his legs, and wore, as he said, "sensible flats" in the kitchen. His temper erupted three or four times a week.

The Haitian prep cook was a gentle guy who smoked dope openly and was known simply as "the Haitian." He constantly walked the shoreline searching for the Floridian's dream—a lost bale of marijuana floating on the tide.

The longest-term employee was a waiter named Grimmes, who always wore his white shirt and black pants. He'd spent so much time trotting to avoid the mosquitoes that he continued the habit indoors. I never heard Grimmes speak and neither had anyone else. He was the subject of much teasing by the only three single women in the swamp, all of whom were named Vickie. General consensus separated them as Vickie Uno, Vickie Dos, and Vickie Tres. One was the gigantic Ur-mother of the primordial swamp. Her breasts began at her throat, descending in a parabola that ended in a mysterious nether region beneath a loose dress. Her chief sidekick was less than five feet tall, and never stopped talking. She always wore the same jeans, with the top unsnapped. The third was older, seemed to be balding, and claimed to have been shot during a burglary.

The three Vickies separated at night according to whim and men, living an extraordinary life for women of plain appearance. They were high priestesses with their pick of consort. They ran in a pack with Rafe and Slim, generating an androgynous sexuality that rivaled the humidity in its permeation of the swamp. All of them smelled of salt, sex, and gin.

Bucky's lieutenant was a blond woman with the straight-wired brain of a reptile. Rose had a crude glass eye in her left socket, and limped on a prosthetic left leg. The Haitian was so terrified of her that if someone mentioned her name, he immediately made the sign of the cross, removed his belt, and ran it through the loops the opposite way.

Before my arrival, I already had an enemy. Mossy had been the interim Naturalist before someone else could be conned into the job. He was very tall, thin from the waist down, and had six fingers on one hand. Mossy's face and body embodied the myth of America, containing a gene of every immigrant who'd strayed across the Atlantic. Unfortunately, he also retained elements of the landbridge walkers during the Ice Age. A week before, he'd been crawling along a table in the dining room, following a rare insect he couldn't identify. The rest of the employees calmly moved their plates for his passage. He suddenly recognized the bug, stood on the table, and lost the top of his scalp to the ceiling fan. By happenstance, I had called the following day and been hired. Mossy loathed me for having usurped his job.

Several other staff members moved through the swamp in such a peripheral fashion that I never knew them. A steady stream of new employees trickled in daily. Some people lasted a full day, but most turned tail after a few hours. Two were followed and arrested by state police. Like rotgut and rainfall, I'd found my low spot.

The breezeway was an open bridge that connected the main facility to a small park ranger's office. Inside was a large, gridded map for charting the progress of storms from Africa to Florida. The ranger was from the Bronx. He devoted his hours to a tiny radio, trying to follow the Mets.

Initially, life in Flamingo reminded me of a rooming house— inhabited by kooks and outcasts, dice that rolled off the table, wrinkles on the face of God. After a week of breathing the heavy air, I took a different view. We were de-evolved humans who'd chosen proximity to the foundations of our existence, living on neither land nor water, but in a foreign world of both. The transient existence prevented anyone from getting too close. No one asked questions. The choice to live in a swamp implied a past that was somehow worse, therefore worth leaving. The Glades were America's version of the French Foreign Legion, and the meager pay kept us all locked in harness.

I soon lost weight from the steady fare of Cuban prison food. Starch was the mainstay, with canned vegetables boiled to limpness. Rafe's primary concern was storing food that could withstand the humidity, since bread grew mold overnight. There were no dairy products for thirty miles. Breakfast was powdered eggs mixed with water and scrambled to a mortar the color of willow buds. I began eating fruit for every meal.

At peak mosquito time I lounged in the ranger's air-conditioned office, reading pamphlets about the swamp. He could never answer any of my questions. He didn't like the swamp and he didn't like me. I borrowed all his books and learned enough to fool any hapless tourist into believing I knew the area like a Seminole. Two weeks after my arrival, Dirt installed the new engine. My vacation was over. The last day before working the tour boat, I applied a thick layer of mud to my face and hands and entered the mangroves.

I became lost immediately. Tree roots rose beyond my head, their branches forming a dim canopy. A myriad of insects swarmed over the mud, entering my ears, mouth, and nose. Water splashed mysteriously in all directions. Though I'd not taken a dozen steps, it was impossible to discern my trail. Panic doused me like kerosene. I wanted to run and to scream. My perceptions became so lucid that I could feel my sweat straining against the mud filling my pores. I saw nothing except the strange cellular familiarity of wet earth. My boot caught an underwater root and I fell. Mud washed from my face and the mosquitoes attacked. I scrambled to the nearest tree and began climbing, feet slipping on the branches, harsh leaves tearing my face. The tree was small but it merged with a large one and I was able to navigate above the water from tree to tree. A line of sunlight pierced the foliage. I moved closer, lost my foothold, and fell out of the swamp a few feet from where I'd entered.

Two silhouetted figures were walking toward me, one short, one enormous.

"There's your Naturalist," Bucky said. "Be double damned if he ain't the seriousest yet."

I shaded my eyes and looked into the ancient face of Captain Jack.

"Are you a serious-minded man?" he said.

I nodded. He plucked a three-inch chameleon from my shoulder. Holding it between thumb and forefinger, he squeezed its belly until the tiny jaws gaped wide, like a clothespin. He lifted the lizard to his ear and released it. The chameleon clamped its mouth around the captain's earlobe and wriggled its feet wildly in the air. I began to laugh.

"He'll do," the captain said.

Bucky frowned, both hands on his hips, shaking his head. It was the first and only time I saw him unable to produce his managerial grin.

Captain Jack climbed lithely aboard the *Heron* and looked at me as if waiting. His hair was close-cropped, white as salt. His eyes were slits in a sun-creased face. With his chin slightly raised, hooked nose, and fence post posture, he had the air of a Roman statesman.

"Ever been on a boat, kid?" he said.

"No sir."

"You cast off and I'll do the rest."

"Yes sir."

"Were you in the service?"

"No sir."

"Do you call all men 'sir'?"

"Sometimes."

"Why?"

"My father made me."

"Was he in the service?"

"No sir."

He stared at me for nearly a minute. He was really looking, regarding in the older sense of its meaning. When he spoke, his voice was softer than before.

"You don't have to call me 'sir.'"

I unhooked the lines and we moved away from the dock and into the bay. Flamingo's rickety line of buildings looked twice as pathetic from the sea, vulnerable and lonely, as if they'd been beached by tide rather than built by man. We entered a channel and moved inland. The red mangroves leaked tannin that dyed the water the flat color of old blood. Captain Jack slowed the engine to a dull steady pulse. Our passage had curved until we were surrounded by the dark groves.

"What happened to your ears?" I said.

The tips of both were corrugated like sawteeth, red and ragged.

"Healed-up cancer. You get it from the sun reflecting off the ocean."

I looked into the shadowy world of the shore. "We're safe here, I guess."

"Yes," he said. "This is one of the dark places on earth."

The somber landscape slid by. Above the engine's laboring throb came the drone of millions of insects, eating and being eaten, living a life in a single season. Captain Jack stared far ahead, handling the *Heron* by intuition.

"Watch that log, kid."

I followed his gaze forward, seeing only the endless gnarled mangroves and occasional knees of cypress. The boat's wake spread behind us like a turkey's tail fan. I expected to hear the sound of a log striking the bow, thumping the length of the boat and ruining the propeller.

"Port side," he said.

Barely visible in the murky water, a log floated away from us, its knobby surface blending with the swamp. It bumped against a strip of muddy shore and continued to rise. Water drained away as a tapered snout climbed the bank, followed by two stubby legs, a long armored body, two more legs, and a scaled tail that dragged the mud. The alligator began walking parallel to the boat, head high as if proud. I felt both envy and awe. Three hundred million years had passed in the forty seconds I watched it move from water to land.

"Small," Captain Jack said. "Only runs to a six-purser."

We reached Coot Bay, a lagoon soaked in light where butterflies flitted among the branches. Our passage out seemed less foreboding. As we moved into the final turn that opened to the Gulf, an eagle attacked an osprey in the sky. The osprey dropped the fish it was carrying and the eagle snatched it in midair. Captain Jack called the eagle "an aerial rat."

For the next three weeks we traveled into the swamp twice a day. There was a sunset voyage into the Florida Bay, watching the sun fall behind the Gulf, staining the long strips of cloud pink and scarlet. Occasionally dolphins cavorted beside us, blowing funnels of water into the air. The plaintive cry of gulls faded into the dusk.

I stood amidships with binoculars and a portable PA system, identifying birds, trees, the occasional manatee and alligator. My most enthusiastic lecture concerned hurricanes. They arrived an average of every seven years, and the last one of any real force had been in 1926. The Everglades was now severely congested, thick and stagnant. A hurricane acted as a giant cleaning machine, ridding the swamp of overgrowth, depositing new seeds and soil, blowing tropical birds from island to mainland. Nature required hurricanes. They were as necessary and valuable as forest fires in the Northwest.

The ranger gave me a pad of graph paper for mapping the movement of storms. A station in Key West announced weather updates every hour, and Captain Jack lent me a radio. Of three tropical depressions, only one developed into a storm, but it petered out while crossing the Atlantic.

When a tour was canceled due to weather, Captain Jack and I talked. During forty years in the Coast Guard, he had killed three men, only one of whom he regretted. Smuggling was the chief crime. I asked if he knew Spanish and he claimed enough to communicate at sea.

"Let's hear it," I said.

"Cómo se llama? De dónde es? Todo es una mentira. Salga de la barca."

"What's that mean?"

"What's your name? Where are you from? It's all a lie. Get out of the boat."

"What else?"

"Nothing. That's all I ever needed."

The majority of our passengers were European tourists making their first American stop. The French complained that our bread was too soft, the British fretted about malaria, and the Germans hated our beer. One day thirty French people crowded our boat. We moved into the bay and I spotted a log floating along the bank.

Following Captain Jack's bilingual example, I spouted my best French: *"A droit, a droit!* Alligator *a droit!"*

The entire gang reacted as if I'd announced the new Beaujolais was of a wonderful grape. They forced their way to the rail, taking pictures and grunting in polite tones. The boat tilted to starboard. A four-year-old boy leaned over the water, his body between the rails. Slowly his feet rose into the air and I watched his little legs slide overboard. Swift as thought, I vaulted the iron rail and hit the nasty water, my feet brushing the bottom. I grabbed the kid by the hair. Something struck my head and I lost him. Floating beside me lay the life preserver attached to a line. The boy was treading water easily, a better swimmer than his rescuer. I grabbed the life ring and beckoned to the kid, who stuck out his tongue and made a face. I splashed water in his eyes and took him by the throat.

Four men pulled the rope back to the boat. Captain Jack stood with one hand on the tiller and the other holding a pistol that I didn't know he carried. My head banged the hull. I pushed the kid up and he kicked me in the face. By the time I was hauled into the boat, my shirt was stained from a nosebleed. The boy was in his mother's arms.

Captain Jack maneuvered the *Heron* to the dock, where I tethered us to the continent. I thought about the boy who'd fallen off his horse in New York, and wondered if rescuing this kid had squared me with the cosmos. As the passengers disembarked, each one kissed me repeatedly on the cheeks. Captain Jack looked very sad.

"What were you going to do?" I said. "Shoot me if I didn't save him?"

"No," he said. "For sharks."

"What?"

"They get trapped in here when the tide goes out. They can't get past the reef. You jumped in shark water, kid. Damn foolish thing to do."

I tried to sit and missed the bench.

"Get up, kid," he said. "You're all right. My wife will be glad for supper company."

I changed clothes and he drove us through the swamp to Homestead. Occasionally he glanced at me and shook his head. Mrs. Jack was very large and treated me as though I were a son home from college. She served fish stew loaded with vegetables, my first real meal in months. Captain Jack nodded as she talked of her day—the perpetually failing garden, a bridge game partnered with a woman she didn't like, the price of lettuce. There seemed to exist between them a pact regarding communication, perhaps the result of her life spent wondering if he'd come home alive. I complimented the food and asked what it was.

"Shark," she said. "The captain's favorite."

He laughed silently, then took me to a screened-in back porch, where he smoked a pipe. He turned the bowl downside up, a habit from the sea. We didn't talk although I sensed he wanted to. Being inland forced a shift between us, a minor tectonic slip we couldn't bridge. At ten o'clock he said it was time for bed.

He showed me to a room with a life-size poster of John Wayne on the wall. A shelf held a row of model cars and a dusty baseball glove. Propped on a desk was a framed photograph of a young face, stoic in a Marine dress uniform. Beside it lay a small box. Captain Jack nodded to the photograph.

"My boy died saving three men. Damn foolish thing to do."

He opened the box, which contained a Bronze Star on a faded ribbon. "Fat lot of good it did him," he muttered. "Or his mother." He closed the box, replaced it in the exact spot on the desk, and stepped into the darkness of the hall. "Damn foolish," he said again.

I turned off the light and stood beside the bed for a long time. I undressed, rolled my pants into a ball, slipped them into my shirt for a pillow, and slept on the floor.

The next day the Haitian was gone from the park. He'd been arrested for possession while I'd been at the captain's house, and the scuttlebutt was simple—I had snitched. No one joined me at meals. If I sat with others, they moved. Even Bucky became more formal, slightly distant, as if giving me plenty of lead rope. Captain Jack and I continued to work well together aboard the *Heron*, but talked less. He was gruff and impatient. His son had come between us in a way I never understood. Captain Jack seemed to resent my knowledge of him, the way a man feels anger toward a friend who saved his life.

My official poetry notebook rapidly filled with journal entries. Friendless and stranded as I was, the journal became a prolonged scream into the swamp, the incessant chatter of a man talking to himself. This was my most productive period.

Hot air falling off the African coast had found a low-pressure spot fed by chilly wind. Heat and cold spun into a tropical depression which moved across the Atlantic, gathering force, following the traditional path of storms. I was elated when it achieved storm status and the name of Jacob. Several times a day the radio station in Key West gave its latitude and longitude, which I charted on my small grid. As the storm failed to dissipate, I became more and more hopeful, staying in my room, listening to the radio. The announcer spoke in a slow drawl. He had a habit of pausing between phrases long enough for me to pose a question in anticipation of what he'd say. When I was right, it was as if he'd answered the question and I was conversing with someone.

"Where you broadcasting from, Joe?" I asked.

"This is Joseph Grady in Key West . . ."

"What are you talking about?"

". . . with an update on tropical storm Jacob . . ."

"Okay, where is it?"

". . . four hundred miles offshore with winds at seventy-five miles per hour. The National Weather Service now calls it a hurricane . . ."

I heard a noise outside my window. Half expecting to see a tidal wave pushed by Jacob, I jerked the curtain back. Dirt stood behind the glass. "Narc!" he snarled, showing both his middle fingers.

"Fucking radio narc!" He backed into the darkness, slapping mosquitoes.

Two days later Jacob was sixty miles offshore, bearing for the coast. Life in the park hadn't changed except that the hostility toward me had become quite open after Dirt's discovery of my radio. I ignored everyone and focused on the hurricane. At the ranger station I compared my small chart with the big one on the wall. The numbers matched but the pinpoints on the map were different. My route showed Jacob aimed directly at us, but the wall chart had the hurricane missing Flamingo by two hundred miles. I copied the official numbers onto a new graph, recharted the path, and compared it to the one on the wall. Instead of finding my error, I discovered the ranger's mistake.

I rapped on the office door. The ranger was hunched over his radio, sweaty and tense. I expected Joseph Grady's voice but heard only fuzzy static. The ranger smacked his fist against the desk and moaned.

"Son of a bitch," he said. "They walked him."

I showed him the discrepancy and his face became pale as milk. He swallowed twice.

"I've got to tell the head ranger," he whispered.

The tourists were evacuated. The ranger packed equipment and left at dusk. Bucky decided to wait another forty-eight hours to save the expense of lodging employees in Miami hotels. Jacob moved thirty miles closer. Joe Grady warned that traffic out of the Keys was very heavy, and drivers should be careful. The sky was dark gray, the weather incredibly calm. The surf rose all day.

The next morning, Jacob sprawled like a monster on the horizon. At noon the hurricane's perimeter swept over the swamp in wind and rain. Strange wet leaves pasted themselves to every surface. The water had risen six feet, but it seemed as if the land had sunk. Employees formed a convoy that I was not asked to join. Dirt led the procession into the mangroves.

I went to my room and wrote a will, leaving everything to my brother. I tried to write a poem but couldn't get past the title—"Blue Flamingo." I bundled my journal in a plastic garbage bag, put on a poncho, and carried the package outside. I had never felt so calm. Jacob was closer now. I climbed the superstructure of the breezeway to a roof support. The bay below chopped white, full of sticks. I tied my package behind a steel post facing away from the sea, toward the rest of America.

Years ago, I'd left Kentucky and set into motion a pattern of repetitive exile that had ended by dropping me into a rapidly sinking swamp. I had entered the world to become a man and wound up truly caring about very little. Most of my life had been a sequence of halfhearted attempts at self-destruction. Somehow I'd always scampered away—you can't get me, I'm the gingerbread man. Now I faced a worthy death, a death of honor in the face of a stormy god. I felt as if I'd summoned the hurricane like a farmer calling hogs, or a shaman making rain. Jacob was coming for me and I would meet him freely. Hoka hey.

During a brief period of calm, I heard Dirt's big Harley in the parking lot. Behind it came the cars. I dropped to the catwalk and asked why they'd come back.

"Roads are flooded past my waist," Dirt said.

I looked at Jacob hulking twenty-five miles away. He had turned us into an island. An arm of rain lashed my face. Everyone ran for cover and I began to laugh. No one had rain gear except me.

I stayed on the breezeway past dark and watched Dirt and Slim break into the bar. They made three trips, carrying out beer and liquor by the case, giggling insanely the entire time. The night was black as a cow's insides. Bored by my death vigil and exhausted from tensing against the wind, I left the breezeway. Through an open door to a room I saw several people naked, each holding a bottle of liquor.

I went to my room and woke with the sea twenty feet from my back door. Joe Grady told me the hurricane had stopped sixteen miles from the tip of Florida. I dressed and pulled on my poncho.

Outside, Rafe was calmly vomiting, wearing only a bra. In the dining room two people ate peaches from a can while drinking beer. I fixed a sandwich and walked to the edge of land.

The eye of a hurricane is big enough for planes to fly into. From this central axis extend dozens of spiral arms composed of wind and rain. The farther they are from the hub, the more they blend together. With Jacob's eye so close, each arm was distinct from the rest. As the hurricane spun, one arm after another struck the coast, like spokes in a wagon wheel. Three minutes of incredibly fierce wind brought on a horizontal rain of pellets the size of rocks. The rain stopped abruptly, followed by three minutes of absolute calm between the arms. Then the cycle repeated.

I sat a few feet from the ocean and watched the horizon turn dark on the left side, clear on the right. As the hurricane rotated, the colors switched sides. The sky seemed to spin like a top, flashing black and white. Time moved in a hypnotic cycle of wind rain calm, wind rain calm. The periods of utter calm were the most frightening, a feint before Jacob delivered another blast of power.

A large pelican tried to fly against the wind. Though it was a few feet from me, I could not hear the sound of its heavy wings. The bird appeared suspended in midair, unable to go forward regardless of effort. A sudden gust hurled it to the ground with killing force.

Night arrived early and I returned to the dining room for food. Shards of broken whiskey bottles glittered underfoot. Mold had already begun to form on the half-eaten food that lay on the tables and floor. Someone slept in a corner. Dirt sat in a folding chair like lost royalty in a demented kingdom, legs open to accommodate Vickie Uno on her knees before him. Her head rose and fell. Rafe crouched beside her. "Not bad," he was saying. "Use your neck, not your shoulders."

I made a sandwich, found some carrots, and went to the breezeway. The shadow of my wrapped notebook clung to the steel brace like a cocoon. The lulling calm was at hand, a warm night in the tropics. From the bay below came the sound of the *Heron* steadily banging the dock. The mangroves and ocean blended with the sky in a vast darkness, as if the world had turned inside out to create a cave. Rain battered my poncho like buckshot. Water gushed along the breezeway.

I lifted my hands into the air as wind came from every direction, twisting the poncho around my face. A tremendous gust lifted my feet. My body tipped over the bay, held by wind to the railing, while my legs lifted behind me. For several seconds I hung in the air, waiting for the blast that would crush me like the pelican. I screamed at the hurricane, daring it to come, cursing it for its refusal.

The wind shifted and my legs dropped, knees striking the concrete. Another gust pinned me to the rail. I shrieked, unable to hear myself. The wind slowed as Jacob's tentacle followed its spiral path. In the sudden rain I realized I was crying, utterly frustrated by my failure to be defeated. I went to my room and took a shower for the first time in three days. My eyes hurt from airborne grit. I turned off the radio and lay shivering in bed, disappointed to be stuck with life.

Jacob was gone by morning.

Sunlight sparkled the water beneath a pristine sky. The hurricane had sucked the clouds into its bowels and the air was clear as that of a desert. The water had receded a few feet, leaving sodden mud where grass had been, flecked with debris. The *Heron*'s awning was stripped away. The boat held three feet of water in which a long snake swam from port to starboard, seeking exit. Dead fish lay on land. As I climbed the steps of the breezeway, an alligator walked across the parking lot, tail scraping the tar, an egret in its mouth.

The bay lay motionless, filled with trees, planks, and a dead manatee. I shinnied up the framework for my notebook. It was damp but safe. In the dining room Bucky and Dirt were sweeping the floor. Bucky grinned at me.

"Knew we were fine," he said.

"Shut up," Dirt said. "My head hurts."

Rafe squealed from the kitchen amid the sound of stainless steel pots crashing to the floor. Another voice began yelling in Spanish.

"Grab a broom," Bucky said to me.

"I'm quitting."

"Now's the best time to be here," he said. "No bugs. No tourists. No humidity."

"You owe me for six days."

"The hurricane doesn't count."

I stepped close enough that he couldn't wield the broom.

"It counts," I said.

Bucky tried to grin, then looked at Dirt, who stared at me. Both smelled bad and needed shaves. Their clothes were as dirty as mine.

"Six days' pay," Bucky said. "What's that after room and board? About sixty dollars."

I nodded.

"I'll give you time and a half to help clean up. We got us a triple damn mess here."

I shook my head. Rose stepped through the batwing kitchen doors. Her eye patch was damp.

"You got no way to leave," she said. "If you don't work here, you're nothing but a tourist. You'll have to rent a room."

"How much is a room?"

"About sixty dollars."

Dirt watched me carefully. I looked at the wreckage in the room, knew the park would stink from rotting animals by nightfall. None of it had anything to do with me.

"Okay," I said.

"Okay, what?" said Rose.

"Yeah," Dirt said. "Okay, what?"

His expression was one of genuine curiosity mixed with anger. I looked at him while I spoke, keeping my voice flat. Any trouble would come from him. I didn't really care, but I didn't need a sucker punch either.

"All I want is my pay."

"Suit yourself," the woman said. "Pay him, Bucky. He better be gone by noon."

"He will," Dirt said. "With me. I'll draw my check too. I hate this fucking place."

"Leave and I'll make a phone call," she said. "The state boys'll be waiting on you."

"I'll come straight back here," Dirt said. "I can outrun any car they got and I'll ride my bike across your other leg. If you set me up, it'll be worth it."

She stepped backwards and bumped into the kitchen doors. They swayed in, swung back, and bounced against her. She stumbled on her false leg.

"Bucky," she said. "Fire them."

"Well, I'm afraid they already quit."

He chuckled and Dirt began to laugh. I joined them and we left the dining room together. Bucky paid us cash and shook our hands.

"She won't stay buffaloed long," he said to Dirt. "You better skedaddle."

"If I get caught," Dirt said, "I'll leave you out of it. But tell her she was aiding and abetting."

Dirt roped my backpack to a chrome spiderweb on the motorcycle's sissy bar. He straddled the bike, kicked the starter, and I climbed on the back. He popped a wheelie and we entered the mangroves.

Twice we stopped for snakes and three times for high water. Birds were dead in the boughs of trees. With the moisture gone from the air, the sun illuminated everything with a clarity both frightening and lovely. We passed three rainbows that plunged into the swamp. Coming around a sharp curve, we surprised an alligator herding her young across the road. Dirt braked and swung to the left. As we shot by, one of the babies turned its head. For the merest fraction of a second we looked directly at each other. The little alligator seemed as surprised as I was.

A few miles farther, we stopped for a giant sea turtle slowly dragging its way along the road. Dirt broke a stick and jabbed the turtle toward the water. It left a sinuous path across the tar.

"Fucker's lost," Dirt said

"Why'd you give me a lift?"

"I don't know. Sick of her lording it over me."

"That wasn't a CB in my room."

"I know. I broke in the next day. You're a sick fuck, in there talking to it."

"Nobody else would."

"You were a narc, you'd have left with the ranger. Let's ride. I got to split fast. I'll drop you in town."

We roared into Florida City and stopped for gas. The town looked the same. Dirt unhooked my pack and tossed it to the blacktop.

"Give me your driver's license," he said. "We'll swap."

I frowned, wondering if this was a biker ritual of farewell. Since I didn't own a car, I wouldn't need it anyway.

"If she rolls over on me," he said, "your ID'll get me by for a while. You aren't on the run, are you?"

"Not from the law."

I handed him my license. It was from Kentucky, the last physical evidence of where I'd started. Everything else in my wallet proclaimed me merely American. Dirt straddled his bike and winked at me.

"Don't let your meat loaf," he said.

I watched the proof of who I was drive into the street, turn a corner, and disappear. I checked his license to learn my name. Jesus Christ, I thought, no wonder he goes by Dirt. I suddenly realized that I didn't know where to go. Chris Offutt was driving away on a motorcycle. Someone else stood in a Florida ghost town beneath the terrible burden of freedom.

The old man at the bus station ignored me, as if he'd become accustomed to escapees from the swamp. He spat near a trash can.

"Do you know who I am?" I asked him.

He shook his head. I smiled and called Shadrack collect. When the operator asked who it was from, I checked the driver's license again.

"Clarence," I said.

He refused but I broke in, saying, "It's me, it's me," and Shad accepted the charge.

"You got room for me?" I asked.

"When?"

"Three days probably. I'm coming by bus."

"You can stay at my dump for twelve hours."

"That's all I could take of seeing that trash you paint."

"I don't paint anymore, Chris. I quit to write my memoir. You'll be a key character. I don't have time for this."

"Okay, bye."

"Wait, Chris. There's one more thing."

"What?"

He hung up, the oldest joke between us.

The bus north was a rumbling gray coffin, evidence of my failure, like a tamed and crippled raptor. We passed a hitchhiker and I ducked, unwilling to see the disdain on his face. Returning to Boston was the first time I'd ever gone back anywhere. For a decade my motto had been "Always Forward," but that had taken me to a swamp and reduced me to a bus. Forward had become backwards.

I had six dollars when Shadrack met me in Boston. He kept remembering money he'd borrowed in the past, enough to keep me in cigarettes and food. He also deigned to share with me the towel I'd given him. I found work at a one-hour photo store, producing imagery before the sentiment had time to fade. Since I was the only male and the only white, customers assumed I was the manager. I quit, tired of people believing lies about me. I wasn't an actor, painter, playwright, or poet. I was just one more nondescript person on the planet. Ponce de León died from a Seminole's arrow at age sixty, still trying to live the life of a youth. I would not make his mistake. I moved into an upscale rooming house and wrote some poems.

A few months blurred by and I met a woman. Rita was a psychologist and musician. She was attractive in an honest way, rather than a gender contraption of makeup, diet soda, and designer jeans. Her body was simply her body, not kneaded by Nautilus into a sculptor's plaster form. Her eyes were enormous and in constant motion. She was far more intelligent than I. She was Calliope making do with a mortal.

Rita asked me to take her out of town, and though I'd lived in the Boston area for years, the only place I felt confident of finding was Salem. The House of Seven Gables has a secret passage that tourists can be led through for a fee. We held hands in that narrow space between the two worlds of past and present. I wanted to kiss her but the guide was hurrying us along.

Later I showed her my poetry and she told me they weren't poems but only looked like them. We had our first fight, which ended when she suggested I write prose. I taught her to drive a car, play poker, and shoot pool. Rita returned me to the species with a careful formula of protection and guidance. I ate and slept in regular patterns. I gained weight.

Within two years we moved three times, first to her hometown of Manhattan, where we were married. Rita had no brother, and her parents considered me a son. We saved some money and moved to Eastern Kentucky. My family welcomed Rita like royalty. They were pretty sure that with her around, I wouldn't wind up in prison or dead.

After a year in the hills, we had run through our savings in a failed attempt to renovate a small house, having gotten as far as adding on a bathroom. Neither of us found work. The journal had become useless, an obvious dodge. With nothing but the familiar around me, I resorted to fiction.

Rita had long urged me to go to a writing school but I refused, afraid to learn that I had no talent. Of all my imagined artistic enterprises, writing was the only one at which I'd made genuine effort. I had three stories, all written in Kentucky, on my home hill.

Broke and in debt, I applied to several graduate programs, choosing the schools on a geographical basis. Rita favored the desert of Arizona and I wanted the Montana mountains. A teacher at the local college suggested that I apply to the University of Iowa, which I did, although the prospect of living on such terrain didn't excite me. Iowa was the first to respond, with an acceptance.

A month later we took out a promissory note and rented a van. I was leaving home again, abandoning the hills. I'd never really found a place in the outside world, but had stayed away too long to fit in at home. We drove twelve hours with my stories in an envelope on my lap. The closer we got to Iowa, the worse the stories seemed. I'd had to reenter the hills to start writing, and I wondered if I'd be able to continue on flat land.

We camped by the Coralville Reservoir until we found an apartment in a condemned building beside the jail. The first year was hard and I considered leaving, an old pattern. Rita convinced me otherwise. We moved to a house by the river, where I built a small room to write in. I had my goddess. I had my temple. The prairie spread in every direction.

The baby is two weeks overdue, a sign of intelligence. It prefers the safety of further percolation instead of expulsion into the world of light and air, sorrow and joy. Lately it has been still, grown too large for its space. Rita's belly is an immense full moon, her navel a smudge pulled inside out. Her lovely breasts rest high on her belly. She can barely walk.

This is the last day of waiting. I slept three hours last night, anesthetized by a half-pint of bourbon. I suffer no hangover this morning, only a wide-eyed dread of a stillbirth. There is no reason to think this way; Rita is in fine health. She has not broken her ban on caffeine, alcohol, and nicotine. I feel odd for leaving her every morning but she urges me out of the house. The only time she gets full rest is when I'm gone. A faint snow filters through the sky. Mist in the trees is actually chimney smoke, held to the earth by impending weather.

The riverbank is a crouching porcupine, bare tree limbs quilling the sky. A pin oak hit by lightning hangs at a right angle like a jack-in-the-pulpit. I crouch within the overhang, a pipeless Pan, Adam before Lilith, a druid needing no specific oak. Tiny beads of snow settle into the folds of cloth at my elbow. The wilderness accepts me as an extension of itself, an arm that knows its hand. I become as old and cold as all the silent trees along the river's edge, accepting snow.

Unless birth occurs today, the hospital will induce Rita's labor tomorrow. Such a timetable is usually reserved for jobs and sporting events. Only war and birth erupt on their own, preemptive strikes of broken water and treaties.

Wind on the surface makes the river appear to flow backwards. I cup my hands and emit the barred owl's call. One answers and I don't respond, satisfied with sharing the dawn. The final count-down has begun. We are like a stakeout team breaking surveillance to catch the baby in the act.

I fear the loss of independence although I didn't do so well alone. What passed for adventure was despair, my courage actually a refusal to acknowledge fear. This arrangement of safety ends to-morrow. I will learn the vocabulary of a father—when you get older, maybe later, ask your mother.

Below the oak lies the regurgitated gray pellet of an owl. After eating its prey whole, an owl expels the bones and fur in a tidy package. This one is very hard, which means it's old. I break it open to find the flat skull of a baby snake. As a child, I was scared of snakes and I intend to teach my kid otherwise. Children are only afraid of what their parents fear, that and the parents themselves.

Beside me the river moves south to join the Cedar, pushing to-ward the Mississippi, flowing to the Gulf. Everything runs to the Gulf. Rita has lightened. The baby's head has wedged into the pelvic exit. Tomorrow the baby will join the earth as a trickling creek. We prepared ourselves four weeks ago in case the baby came early. Already it has fooled its folks.

I leave the woods and cross the yard to check on the boat. Months back, I pulled it into the yard to save it from the crush of ice. The boat looks bigger on land than in the water. I sit on the middle seat. Woodsmoke pushes down, swirling around me, the sign of a coming storm. The raw cry of a crow kills the silence, drawing my attention. An eagle stands on one leg in a tree, holding a bloody fish in its other claw, darting its head to rip through the scales. Crows land in nearby boughs as if paying homage to the superior hunter. They remind me of children trying to learn, and it occurs to me that fathers always seem to be of a different species.

I stay as long as I can against the cold. Tree limbs curve to the earth beneath the weight of snow. Every second brings me closer to fatherhood. I'm waiting in a boat on land, surrounded by smoke that does not rise. The river is flowing upstream.

The alarm clock buzzed at dawn. I fought exhaustion until the reason for such an early morning released enough adrenaline to melt dry ice. The outside air was dark as dusk. Rita's preternatural eyes gleamed, anticipating relief. Maternity and paternity possessed the supremely differing points of view of a shaman and a televangelist, a proton and an electron, a quarterback and the football itself. Neither of us could eat breakfast. Mist from the river rose to blend with snow, the earth and sky mixing in air.

I held Rita's arm as we walked to the car. The sun was beginning to rise, with the moon still hung in the west. I stood between the two companions of the planet, feeling the lure of each, the myth of both. Earth was the broker of life while the moon marked passage of time. I drove slowly, carefully. We didn't speak. At the hospital an orderly whisked Rita away in a wheelchair, her belly leading the way. Fifteen minutes later a nurse pecked my shoulder.

"Are you the acting father for Mrs. Offutt's child?"

"The husband."

She frowned at her clipboard. "This way," she said.

"What do you mean, acting father?"

"Birth coach."

I followed her through an elaborate security system to the delivery room, where Rita lay connected to a coil of wires and cords. A blood pressure gauge wrapped her left arm. She wore a belt that monitored the fetus through electrodes fastened to her body. A machine charted contractions with a tiny stylus like a seismograph. The spindly IV dripped Pitocin, a hormone that would eventually trigger labor.

I asked the nurse about alternatives to Pitocin.

"Nipple stimulation sometimes helps but I'm afraid it's two weeks too late."

"You're afraid?" I said.

From down the hall came an anguished howling. The nurse hurried away and I envisioned our neighbor having just seen the two-headed freak she'd emitted from her body. I pulled the deck of cards from our suitcase and offered Rita a cut. We played gin rummy and I won handily. Rita tried to doze. I left for a walk and discovered a herd of stark-eyed men biting lips, nails, and cuticles. One man twitched uncontrollably; another scratched his forearm with the methodic repetition of a lunatic. Conversation consisted of grunts and swallows. Eventually we were all driven away by a sweaty bastard who delivered a monologue on the three previous babies his wife had lost. If this one didn't come, he was filing for divorce.

I visited the nursery, where eight babies were wrapped like mummies in transparent cribs. A tiny girl lay beneath heat lamps, and I recalled a psychology class field trip to a center for children abandoned to the state. Room after room contained naked idiots. At puberty they had to be taught to masturbate; otherwise they dry-humped furniture and smaller kids. The prize was a hydrocephalic nine-month-old with a head the size of a wheelbarrow, flattened by gravity from lying on its side. The four skull plates were clearly delineated as if floating beneath the surface.

I left quickly. Nurses were joking behind a low barricade that reminded me of a strip club's protective bar. I wanted a drink. I settled beside Rita to read poetry but was unable to concentrate. While she slept, I took another tour of the labyrinth and peeked in the cesarean room, a regal chamber with the atmosphere of a scrubbed crypt. It was empty save for a shiny metal table beneath a giant bank of lights. In the waiting room I found a spy novel and moved through it with ease.

Four hours later Rita's contractions increased and I was very hungry. The sandwiches we'd stored in the suitcase a month ago were moldy. While trying to aid her through latent labor, I felt more like a cheerleader than a coach. Mainly I wanted each thirty-second contraction to end so I'd have ten free minutes to read my thriller. A high-ranking official was suspected of being a mole and the protagonist had a gunshot wound in his upper thigh. Rita was moaning. Every half hour a nurse checked her cervical dilation and effacement.

Rita entered the second stage of active labor, and I couldn't find my flashcards. She squirmed in pain. I was powerless and frustrated, capable only of holding her hand and counting to five as she thrust breath from her lungs in harsh increments. I called a friend and asked for food. An hour later a nurse brought in a duffel bag containing tuna on whole wheat and an airline bottle of whiskey. Between contractions, I ate the sandwich and promptly vomited into the bag, trying to conceal it from Rita. My sensitivity was wasted. She didn't notice.

The second stage was running long and our doctor dropped by to increase the Pitocin from one drop per minute to two. She asked how I was doing, then patted me on the head. A nurse ran an electrode into Rita's vagina and fastened it to the baby's skull. Rita refused medication. She was determined to nurse her baby in a coherent manner immediately following birth. She breathed and grunted, expending more energy than a sumo wrestler. Her eyes stayed shut. I mopped sweat from her face and fed her slivers of ice dipped in juice. Time slid into an oblivion of one-minute cycles that reminded me of the hurricane—breath push rest, breath push rest. The computer graph peaked and troughed in a record of Rita's work. The room faded into a bathysphere containing the two of us, connected at the palms. Later I learned she'd undergone hard labor for six hours.

Suddenly the room filled with medical personnel summoned by a machine at the nurses' station. The monitor showed infant distress—each contraction was lowering the fetal heartbeat. A nurse shouldered me aside and dropped a hidden trapdoor in the bed between Rita's legs. Someone placed a wide-mouthed bucket below.

My mouth was dry. The cervix was dilated to the maximum of ten centimeters, fully effaced, soft as dough. A nurse brought a pair of giant gleaming salad tongs on a steel tray. The doctor inserted one, then the other, clipped them together at the handle, and began maneuvering them by feel and memory. Everyone's brow was wet. I could do nothing but wipe Rita's face and hold her hand.

The doctor called for a specialist, a jolly fellow with massive forearms. He ran the forceps in and strained until his knuckles whitened, shifted his body slightly, and removed the slimy instruments. He nodded to our doctor and strode away. I imagined a baby with a head shaped like an hourglass. Everyone began talking at once. The doctor crouched in a three-point stance between Rita's legs and shouted, "Push it out, push it out!" Liquid splatted into the metal bowl.

"Crowning," a nurse said. "It's crowning."

"Heartbeat down," said another.

"Fetal distress."

"Episiotomy."

"Cord around its neck. Cord around its neck."

I glanced down and saw a dark red sphere emerging from Rita's abdomen. She was shrieking. I turned my head.

"It's gone, it's gone."

I looked back and what had been the baby's head had indeed disappeared, sucked back inside. Everyone was yelling instructions. I leaned to Rita's ear and murmured words that emerged as gibberish.

"Here it comes," the doctor said. "Crowning, crowning."

Again I saw the head appear like a turtle's from a shell, then retreat.

"Danger of asphyxiation."

"Prepare for cesarean."

"It's coming back."

"Push! Push! Push!"

Through the terror and intensity of the moment, I felt an odd respect for the fetus. After being squeezed through a tight tunnel for a quick view, it had opted for return, prolonging the safety of darkness and food. It was certainly my kid.

"Episiotomy, quick."

"It's tearing, it's tearing."

"Push, push, push. Here it comes."

"Good good good good good good."

Its face emerged in profile between Rita's legs. Circled around its neck was a pale fleshy cord like a snake. The doctor cut the umbilicus, which flipped onto Rita's stomach as if sentient and alive, settling slowly into her deflating skin. From the vicinity of her pelvis came a strangled sound.

"There it is!"

"It's out! It's out!"

The doctor placed a wet mounded lump on Rita's stomach, aimed at her breasts. The baby didn't look like what the books had described. There was no cheesy substance, and the head wasn't elongated. The thing was gray and wrinkled as old meat. It didn't move. In that moment, I was sure that it was dead.

"My baby," Rita said. "My baby, my baby."

A tubular arm wiggled from beneath its head and stretched into the air, bending at the elbow, tiny fingers moving in a clutching motion. Just as quickly, the arm retracted. I leaned closer—no tail, a full head of dark, bloody hair. It looked like an Aleut after a vicious alley fight, with puffy eyes and scuff marks on its cheeks. The hands were fisted at the ready.

"Boy," said a nurse. "It's a boy."

She scooted him forward and guided his mouth to Rita's nipple.

"Sutures," the doctor said. "Bring extra fast."

A nurse gathered the baby and carried it to the far side of the room. She weighed him, measured his length like a fish, and ran her fingers in his mouth.

"Good palate," she called. "All ten fingers and toes. Nine on the Apgar." She turned to me. "Watch this."

She held him beneath his armpits and slowly lowered his feet until they touched the surface of a sterile table. A leg lifted in an immediate step.

"Only humans do that at birth," she said. "It's my favorite part."

She laid him on the table, rolled him in a blanket like a burrito, and offered him to me.

"He can't be with the mother while she's having surgery," she said. "It wouldn't be safe."

I took him stiffly and we stared at each other. His eyes were deep blue, his hands gigantic. A cleft in his chin astounded me. I identified myself and welcomed him. He'd become pink but remained quite mute, his vision locked to mine. It occurred to me that he knew mysterious things. I could see an awareness that was at once exhilarating and frightening. I wanted him to speak, to tell me everything. What he'd just experienced was fresh in his mind, soon to be buried except for nightmares. We stared for many minutes, passing unknown information back and forth through the conduit of his initial sight. I cried and sang to him. Nine months of fear spiraled away. His birth was my rebirth. Paternal terror was simply ignorance. The baby knew everything there was to know.

I became aware of an eerie high-pitched moan, a battlefield keening. The doctor sat on a stool between Rita's legs. Rita writhed on her back, head swinging side to side, her hair a constant dark motion. Two nurses held her arms. For an hour she moaned, receiving ninety-four stitches. At the last second of birth our baby had lowered his shoulder and forced his way into the strange world of light and space.

I carried him to his mother but Rita was in a private zone of pain and joy. The nurse motioned me away. I made the mistake of checking the doctor's work. Her smock was bright red, the sewing finally complete. The doctor dipped her hands into the bucket and lifted what appeared to be a plastic dry-cleaning bag. She turned it inside out, gauging viscosity and content. I thought of augury, of pagan belief in the potency of the amnion. Satisfied, the doctor dropped it and red water splashed the floor. My knees felt weak and I was very scared of dropping the baby. I imagined my arms to be iron bars.

A nurse took the baby and presented it to Rita. She was cooing like an animal. I dug through the duffel bag and drained the tiny bottle of emergency whiskey. I sat in a chair, staring at the living symbol of life, Isis and Ra, woman and child.

The doctor reappeared in fresh clothes. A nurse sponged Rita and draped her in a clean gown. Everyone was smiling. Another nurse asked me his name. Over the sound of conversation came the baby's cry. Rita's nipple had slipped askew. She adjusted it and everyone listened to the baby's quick breath, the suckling sound, the tiny mewing of life.

Epilogue

My son is three months old and on my back, strapped in a red harness. Today is the first day of spring, his first visit to the woods. His chubby legs bounce against my back. Seventeen years have elapsed since the last locust outbreak and the forest floor is full of finger-size holes. The earth has given the insects to light. Their drone rises and falls around us like distant chain saws. Rita is home, grateful for some time alone. Our son sleeps between us in the bed, and at night I arrange myself in order to hold his hand.

Flocks of starlings migrate along the river. The softwoods bud, the hardwoods wait. My family and I talk more often on the phone. Dad inquires about the "son of my son." I ask him what he wants the kid to call him. "Grandfather," he says. "That way he'll always know there's someone grander than his father."

My mother wants to know who he resembles and I tell her he looks like himself, realizing later that the same phrase is used to describe a corpse lying in state. We live far away from them. I grew up not seeing my grandparents and have always regretted the loss. Now it would seem the pattern repeats.

The load on my back weighs nothing and everything. I stop to shift him, and feel a vine on my leg, around my boot. It is a tiny garter snake. Behind its head is a yellow stripe the size of a wedding ring. I pick it up gently, knowing that children accidentally kill them through gleeful handling. I turn my head to my son and hold the snake over my shoulder. His little fingers float toward it, pull back.

The river is high from flood to the north. Rita and I are always sleepy. Six weeks after the birth, our doctor sanctioned making love, but our son interrupted us the first few times. It seemed fitting somehow and I didn't mind the halt. I was worried that Rita would feel different to me, that birth had transformed her passage. Her breasts had already become utilitarian, functioning independent of aesthetics. Making love to a maiden is one thing, to a mother quite another. When our son slept, Rita and I molded together, pressing as much flesh against each other as possible. My fears shed as easily as autumn leaves in rain. Nothing had changed except everything.

I come to a downed tree and remove the pack containing my son. The pack has an aluminum bar that folds forward so it can stand alone. It is bigger than him and he slumps sideways, listing like a trawler. I straighten him and he slides the other way. No matter how I try, he cannot sit straight, but his eyes the color of mine never leave my face. I sit cross-legged before him. The woods are heavy around us. The equinox signals the beginning of life and crop, of nesting birds and mating animals. I want to explain everything. I want to tell him what to do, and more important, what not to do. I give him a leaf which he calmly tastes. He can't learn from my mistakes, only from his own.

I think of all the things I want to tell him, and say nothing. According to my father, I come from a long line of bad fathers, improving with each generation. The birth of my son has made me a middleman, nearer to death and to life, closer to my father. With courage and work, my son will become an adult one day. Amid the trees and birds, I realize that despite the obstacles I set myself, I have somehow become one myself.

I press my forehead to the forehead of my son. His tiny brow is warm. I can see his fontanel pulsing with life. Daddy loves you, is all I can think to say. Like all sons before him, he says nothing. The woods enclose us like a tent. The river flows beside us and touching it means touching the sea.

FOR THE BEST IN PAPERBACKS, LOOK FOR THE

In every corner of the world, on every subject under the sun, Penguin represents quality and variety—the very best in publishing today.

For complete information about books available from Penguin—including Pelicans, Puffins, Peregrines, and Penguin Classics—and how to order them, write to us at the appropriate address below. Please note that for copyright reasons the selection of books varies from country to country.

In the United Kingdom: For a complete list of books available from Penguin in the U.K., please write to *Dept E.P., Penguin Books Ltd, Harmondsworth, Middlesex, UB7 0DA.*

In the United States: For a complete list of books available from Penguin in the U.S., please write to *Consumer Sales, Penguin USA, P.O. Box 999— Dept. 17109, Bergenfield, New Jersey 07621-0120.* Visa and MasterCard holders call 1-800-253-6476 to order all Penguin titles.

In Canada: For a complete list of books available from Penguin in Canada, please write to *Penguin Books Canada Ltd, 10 Alcorn Avenue, Suite 300, Toronto, Ontario, Canada M4V 3B2.*

In Australia: For a complete list of books available from Penguin in Australia, please write to the *Marketing Department, Penguin Books Ltd, P.O. Box 257, Ringwood, Victoria 3134.*

In New Zealand: For a complete list of books available from Penguin in New Zealand, please write to the *Marketing Department, Penguin Books (NZ) Ltd, Private Bag, Takapuna, Auckland 9.*

In India: For a complete list of books available from Penguin, please write to *Penguin Overseas Ltd, 706 Eros Apartments, 56 Nehru Place, New Delhi, 110019.*

In Holland: For a complete list of books available from Penguin in Holland, please write to *Penguin Books Nederland B.V., Postbus 195, NL-1380AD Weesp, Netherlands.*

In Germany: For a complete list of books available from Penguin, please write to *Penguin Books Ltd, Friedrichstrasse 10-12, D-6000 Frankfurt Main 1, Federal Republic of Germany.*

In Spain: For a complete list of books available from Penguin in Spain, please write to *Longman, Penguin España, Calle San Nicolas 15, E-28013 Madrid, Spain.*

In Japan: For a complete list of books available from Penguin in Japan, please write to *Longman Penguin Japan Co Ltd, Yamaguchi Building, 2-12-9 Kanda Jimbocho, Chiyoda-Ku, Tokyo 101, Japan.*